Culture Warrior

Also by Bill O'Reilly
available from Random House Large Print

The No Spin Zone: Confrontations with the Powerful and Famous in America

Who's Looking Out for You?

Those Who Trespass: A Novel

BILL O'REILLY

★ ★ ★ ★ ★ ★ ★ ★ ★ ★ ★ ★ ★ ★ ★ ★ ★ ★ ★

Culture Warrior

RANDOM HOUSE
LARGE PRINT

Published in the United States of America
by Random House Large Print in association
with Broadway Books, New York.
Distributed by Random House, Inc., New York.

Page 311 constitutes an extension
of this copyright page.

Library of Congress Cataloging-in-Publication Data
O'Reilly, Bill.
Culture warrior / by Bill O'Reilly.—1st large print ed.
p. cm.
Originally published: New York:
Broadway Books, 2006.
ISBN-13: 978-0-375-43505-8
ISBN-10: 0-375-43505-0
1. United States—Social conditions—1980-
2. Social values—United States. 3. Mass media—
Social aspects—United States. I. Title.
HN65.O74 2006
306.0973'09045—dc22
2006024729

www.randomlargeprint.com

FIRST LARGE PRINT EDITION

10 9 8 7 6 5 4 3 2

This Large Print edition published in accord
with the standards of the N.A.V.H.

This book is dedicated to the men and women who are serving, or have served, in the Armed Forces of the United States. Warriors in defense of justice and freedom, because of you, I am free to write these words.

CONTENTS

CONTENTS

CONTENTS

PART 3: The Struggle for the Soul of America

There are, in the body politic, economic and social, many and grave evils, and there is urgent necessity for the sternest war upon them.

—**Theodore Roosevelt**

Culture Warrior

Central Command (CENTCOM) Initial Briefing

At times you **have** to fight. No way around it. At some point, every one of us is confronted with danger or injustice. How we choose to combat that challenge is often life-defining. You can face difficulties head-on, or run from them, or ignore them until they consume you. But no one escapes conflict. No one.

In my experience of more than thirty years of practicing journalism, I've found that most people do not like to fight. No surprise there. Battle is not only exhausting and dangerous; it also requires skill and discipline to emerge victorious, much less unscathed.

That's why few of us, except for some weirdly self-destructive souls, seek out conflict. In fact, putting yourself at risk goes against our natural impulse of self-preservation. Whenever I've witnessed strife, I've met far more villains than heroes, but both are relatively rare. Most human beings are neither heroes nor villains but decent people who choose to sit things out until pushed beyond a reasonable limit.

For a variety of reasons that I will explain, I have chosen to jump into the fray and become a warrior in the vicious culture war that is currently under way in the United States of America. And war is exactly the right term. On one side of the battlefield are the armies of the traditionalists like me, people who believe the United States was well founded and has done enormous good for the world. On the other side are the committed forces of the secular-progressive movement that want to change America dramatically: mold it in the image of Western Europe. Notice I did not say anything about "conservatives against liberals." This is not the real culture fight, as I'll make clear. The talk-radio mantra of the left versus the right doesn't even come close to defining the culture war in America—it is much more complicated than that.

Rather surprisingly, at least to me, one result of my decision to fight in this war has been financial success. Another result has been a measure of fame. Chances are you know who I am and what I do. But you may not understand **why** I do what I do. That, as they say on TV, is coming up.

The culture war has also made me perhaps the most controversial broadcaster in the country. That hot-button label "controversial" gives my enemies, they think, the right to attack me and my enterprises ceaselessly, unfairly, even dementedly. I truly drive the opposing force nuts! As you may know, I'm engaged in fighting them on a daily basis, and that warfare is the subject of this book.

Maybe it helps that many of my Irish ancestors were warriors. They lived in County Cavan and fought Oliver Cromwell when he devastated Ireland in the name of the British Commonwealth. They lost that fight. Later, some of them emigrated to America during the great famine of the 1840s. More came later. My paternal grandfather fought in World War I, then became a New York City police officer. He was one tough SOB. I have his billy club in my desk drawer. It was well used. Come to think of it, maybe I was named after that club.

In the next generation's world war, my father was a naval officer and was on the scene during the occupation of Japan. He was by nature a warrior but, in an interesting contradiction, was also frightened by the unknown, the Great Depression having imposed upon my father a fear that he never defeated. Even so, his instincts were to combat injustice and scorn those who ran from necessary conflict. But his reluctance to challenge authority and take chances in his career and life would stifle his potential. I watched throughout my growing years as he was slowly beaten down by the system. The problem was that Dad was very bright and creative, but his job converting foreign currency into dollars was pure drudgery. My father died young, at age sixty-two. Observing him, I vowed never to allow the "system" to beat me or to let any individual push me around as his direct superiors did him.

So far, I'm ahead on that score.

I can tell you truthfully that I never envisioned myself crusading against establishment forces like the **New York Times** and today's vast armies of far-left and far-right zealots. Coming out of Boston University with a master's degree in broadcast journalism in 1975, I wanted to be one of the Woodward and Bernstein guys. You know, do serious investigative work and right wrongs by exposing corruption. I also wanted to cover war and study human conflict first-hand. In my journalistic career, I succeeded in reaching those goals and count myself very fortunate to have done so.

Then life, as it usually does, presented me with a completely unanticipated opportunity. After having national success on a syndicated program called **Inside Edition,** I went back to school. And not just any school: At the age of forty-six, I earned a master's degree in public administration from Harvard's Kennedy School of Government. It was while studying in Cambridge, Massachusetts, that I worked up the game plan for **The O'Reilly Factor.** The rest, to use a cliché, is history.

The Factor concept is very simple: Watch all of those in power, including and especially the media, so they don't injure or exploit the folks, everyday Americans. Never before in the United States had a television news guy dared to criticize other journalists on a regular basis. The late Peter Jennings, a friend, told me I was crazy to do it. "These people will not allow anyone to scrutinize them," he said. "They will come after you with a vengeance."

And so they have.

In fact, not since the late Howard Cosell has an American broadcaster been so roundly vilified in print as I have been over the past decade. "Gasbag," "blowhard," "demagogue"—these are common adjectives used when newspaper writers refer to me. I'm not whining, just stating a fact. Because I criticize what I consider to be dishonest and unfair media, and extremist pundits on **both** the right and the left as well as corrupt and/or ineffective politicians, there is no shortage of people trying to marginalize me, or worse, destroy me.

Because of the very personal nature of the battle I have chosen to fight, this is a difficult book to write. I don't like to sound bitter, but the truth is, I **am** bitter to some extent. Although I have won far more battles than I've lost, my life has changed drastically. I am routinely threatened with physical harm and have to employ security. I have to absorb rank defamation in the press, with no legal recourse because I'm a "public figure." My family has also been threatened and I've had to change every aspect of my life. No longer can I behave as a "regular guy" and go out and cut loose with my friends. No longer can I even engage a stranger in conversation—there are too many crazies out there. At work, every call I receive is monitored and every interaction I have has to be witnessed. I am never off the job and am always on guard. Would you want to live that way?

Still, to quote Hyman Roth in **The Godfather II**, "This is the business we've chosen." And it's true. I don't **have** to be a culture warrior. I could make millions doing straight anchor work or just writing books. But I'm on a mission, one that I'm going to define for you throughout this book, and the mission is important.

At this point, all the conflict has been worth it. **The Factor** has changed many things in America and put a horde of bad guys on the defensive and some out of business. Of course, some Americans see **me** as the bad guy. They are entitled to their opinion. But after ten years of unprecedented success, millions of you understand that my programs are trying to fight the good fight. You know the culture war is serious and needs to be fought honestly and effectively. We do that on **The Factor.** And we do it with no fear.

In this book I will try to put the war into perspective. I will try to avoid cheap shots and vindictiveness. This is definitely not a "hit" book written in an attempt to destroy certain people. I'll leave that kind of nastiness to smear merchants like Al Franken and Michael Weiner (aka Michael Savage)—people who try to ruin people in order to make money. It would be foolish and a waste of your time to engage the lunatic fringe in these pages, although the temptation is strong. Occasionally, I'll make an example of a smear merchant to demonstrate a point, but I'll keep that sort of thing to a minimum.

My reasoning is simple: Why dignify slander and libel by repeating them in print? Yes, I do truly despise the ideological fanatics, the media vermin who couldn't care less about truth or justice. But you know who they are. I have bigger, more dangerous targets in my sights—establishment players who can change your life with the stroke of a pen, an activist court ruling, or a dishonest article in the press. My goal is to expose and defeat people who have the power to do you great harm. My weapons will be facts and superior analysis based on those facts. It is absolutely fair and vital to democracy to confront people in the arena of ideas. I'll leave the smears to the yapping character assassins. They will destroy themselves. Just wait and see.

Finally, I want to get back to Howard Cosell for a moment. I consider him one of America's greatest sports commentators, as well as a man who was absolutely fearless in the broadcast booth. If you missed Cosell on the air, consider this: At one point, according to a poll taken by **TV Guide**, he was cited as the most disliked sportscaster in America . . . and also the most **well** liked. In the same poll! Growing up, I had admired his ability to stimulate discussion and provide a vivid, original point of view. He worked without a script, as I often do now. He shouted (I occasionally do that), and he used an extensive vocabulary never before heard in sports broadcasting. It all made an impression on me. I also noticed that my father despised Cosell but watched him every chance he got, complaining about him while enjoying the controversy he engendered.

Shortly before he died in 1995, after being off the air for about ten years, Howard Cosell granted me a rare interview. At that point, his beloved wife had died and he had turned against most of his friends. He had even bitterly denounced his former **Monday Night Football** broadcast partners Frank Gifford and Don Meredith in print.

I met with Cosell in his New York City apartment. He seemed to be a lonely guy and had little good to say about anyone or anything. At the end of the interview, he remarked bitterly: "I don't think another Howard Cosell will ever be allowed in the industry, because they don't want the truth. I mean, the public really doesn't give a damn about the truth."

Well, Howard may have been wrong on both counts. Certainly, **The O'Reilly Factor** is as controversial as anything Mr. Cosell was ever involved with, so today's television industry is open, in some quarters, to strongly stated points of view. And most Americans do want the truth, at least in my experience. My entire presentation is designed to bring you honest information about complicated and important matters (hence the now-famous "No Spin Zone"). Millions of folks are on board with that. In the following pages, we'll continue that mission—bringing the culture war into vivid focus.

One more thing in this initial briefing. We're going to get this culture war over with faster than anyone believes. You've heard of Sun Tzu's **The Art of War**? This ancient Chinese how-to book has been a bestseller in many different formats, especially to people who want to compete more effectively in business.

"There is no instance," wrote the military sage Tzu, "of a country having benefited from prolonged warfare." O'Reilly Tzu agrees (and will have some advice on the subject later on). The culture war must be won quickly and definitively, and the best way to do that is to expose the secular-progressive movement in our country for exactly what it is, to explain why it is so harmful for America, and to identify the movement's top leaders. So here we go.

PART 1

The Conflict: America in the Year 2020?

Excerpts from the State of the Union speech by the President of the United States, Gloria Hernandez:

My fellow Americans, after much hard work, we have finally arrived at a point in our history where we can truly call the United States a diversified nation striving to be at peace with the world. We are well on our way to completing our program of making America a more just, progressive society based upon—secular humanism!

With your help, we have thrown off the narrow-minded, bigoted agenda of those who would use the Constitution to oppress their fellow human beings. Our new programs guarantee that, in the future, we will all share in the prosperity of America equally. Also, we will be able to live our lives as true individuals, without moral limitations imposed by theocrats and others who seek to regulate legal private conduct.

In short, we have come a long way toward fulfilling the mandate of our forefathers. Freedom, yes, but with a policy of generosity toward those who are less fortunate. A true government by the people, and especially **for** the people!

As you know, our opponents are tough and determined to return to the days when the doctrine of so-called self-reliance ruled this country and turned it into a society that primarily benefited the rich. But with the help of the enlightened media, the progressive philosophy of shared assets and a strong platform of individual rights has become the prevailing wisdom in America, and I am proud to be its standard-bearer.

Just think what we've been able to achieve in the past two years. We have begun a system of progressive taxation—**assets**, not just income—that will redistribute wealth from the very few to the many. No longer will any American be denied health care, or a decent place to live, or nutritious food on the table. These are rights, not options. And every American is entitled to those rights.

The new Progressive Initiative on Taxation (PIT) that caps an American citizen's net worth at $15 million achieves an essential goal: Now the federal government will finally have the financial ability to provide security to all citizens, no matter what situation they may find themselves facing. The government will make sure that no one is excluded from the American dream.

Billions of dollars in taxed private assets will flow into the U.S. Treasury over the next few years, and those assets will be used to fund programs like the "Property Enhancement Initiative," where poor Americans are provided with new homes virtually mortgage-free. The construction of these houses will provide a dramatic boost to the economy and slums will become nonexistent. This is one of many programs we have designed under the banner of "shared prosperity."

This year alone, more than $75 billion of new revenue derived from our new Fair Annual Tax (FAT) plan will be awarded to less-well-off Americans to ensure their Constitutional rights. That revenue will double over the next five years as America's new taxation system becomes complete.

And it gets even better. As you know, the Supreme Court has upheld our new progressive taxation system, including the seizure of "surplus personal assets," and it has also upheld a myriad of long-overdue individual human rights. Repressive laws against gay marriage, euthanasia, personal drug use, underage and late-term abortions, and most private sexual preferences have been struck down, as well as all laws that limit freedom of expression. No longer will any American be persecuted for pursuing happiness in his or her own way in the privacy of his or her own home. From now on, the United States will be an example of tolerance and inclusiveness to the entire world.

But, my fellow Americans, perhaps most important, America is leading the way on championing the rights of children. No longer will there be government-mandated school testing in the public schools. Each student will be free to choose his or her own curriculum, and to graduate from high school on an equal footing with everyone else. No child will be saddled with a subjective grading system, either. Diplomas will reflect student participation and pursuit of excellence **as the individual student sees it**. We have truly set the American child free to learn what is most beneficial to her or him. My doctrine of personal happiness for all Americans, including children, is a cornerstone of the secular-progressive movement.

Ladies and gentlemen, we have come a long way in a short time, but we have much more to do. My administration is committed to creating a country in which each individual is truly equal. No majority will ever oppress a minority again, and that includes in the religious arena. As you know, the Supreme Court has ruled that religious expression is to be prohibited in the public square; we have truly now achieved separation of church and state. While spirituality is appropriate in houses of worship, it is not to be used as a coercive instrument in public. My administration is determined to nurture all Americans by protecting them from judgments they may find offensive made by third parties under the name of religion. Remember, more wars have been fought over religion than any other subject. Thus, the words "In God We Trust" are no longer on United States currency. In the new America, you are free to trust in God but not to insist that your fellow citizen share that trust.

Looking to the outside world, my administration will continue to fight for open borders and unfettered free trade, because the entire world community should have access to the prosperity that, by chance, has thrived in America. We must be a generous people and commit to developing one world where decisions are made by nations working in harmony for the good of all. No longer can America expect to be the sole superpower on this earth. That is counterproductive and selfish. We are all of the human race, inhabiting one planet. We are all in this together, and exclusion can no longer be a policy for America.

While it is true that armed conflicts continue to rage in Asia and the Middle East, my administration, in cooperation with the United Nations, continues to believe that justice and peace will be brought to mankind through the implementation of the one-world concept. I am convinced that the shifting of our foreign policy from unilateralism to a multinational strategy of "reasoned engagement" will result in more security for America and every other lawful nation.

Spurred on by religious fanaticism, rogue countries and movements continue to attack innocent civilians here and all over the world through the use of cowardly terrorist actions. Our new plan of international cooperation will isolate these terrorists and bring the perpetrators of violence to justice in the World Court, located at The Hague. We may suffer casualties in the short term, but rest assured, we will win this struggle and see world peace in our lifetimes.

The recent attacks on American soil are but a small price to pay for a vision that will lead to peace and harmony on this planet. All great things require suffering, but we will prevail. Our secular-progressive, one-world vision will triumph over the doubters and evildoers, of that I am sure.

Finally, to those who disagree with the progressive vision that has taken root in America, I reach out and hope you will join us. There is no place in this country for greed, bias, judgmental behavior, aggression, religious zealotry, or exclusionary policies. We are all brothers and sisters on this planet, and we should act as such. For far too long, traditionalists, conservatives, and other misguided Americans have encouraged division by religious and economic philosophies that lead to exclusion and suffering and income inequality. Those antiprogressive forces are still among us, but they are rapidly losing influence to the enlightened followers of secular humanism.

The new world order has indeed arrived, and I am proud to be the one to lead America into the promised land of collective prosperity and true freedom. Thank you, my fellow Americans, and may shared generosity bless America.

One

Armies of the Night

> Me? A cold warrior? Well, yes—if that is how they wish to interpret my defense of values.
>
> —MARGARET THATCHER

President Hernandez is unquestionably a woman of deeply held convictions. That should be obvious to anyone reading her address to the nation. But, because she is committed to the secular-progressive agenda, she sees America in a far different way than the Founding Fathers saw it, although she would never admit that.

The goals and philosophies that the President so enthusiastically stated are all in play right now in America, every one of them.

Let's recap:

- A sharing of the wealth by targeting the affluent for most of the government's revenue.

- Lax school discipline on American children to promote their so-called liberties.
- Naked hostility to religious values and their expression in public.
- A "one-world" approach to foreign relations that would prevent the U.S. government from imposing a policy that would benefit America first.
- A touchy-feely vision of our society that places individual self-expression and rights over self-sacrifice and adult responsibility.

No politician today would dare state this secular-progressive program openly, because the country is not ready for this agenda. But believe me: The vision articulated by President Hernandez is on the drawing board. The armies of secularism are rising and the public is largely unaware of what is taking place.

If you pay attention to the culture wars, it is clear who the shock troops are: The American Civil Liberties Union (ACLU) is the vanguard, waging a war of legal maneuvers designed to ensure secular policies without having to go to the ballot box. In the past ten years, thousands of ACLU lawsuits have blitzed the legal system, almost all of them designed to promote progressive causes and banish traditional ones.

A few far-left billionaires finance the progressive shock troops—millions have poured into the ACLU war chest as well as into the pockets of Internet smear merchants who engage in character assassinations of perceived opponents.

The online character assassins also make good use of the mainstream print media, which are about three-quarters progressive, by my estimation. The level of ideological commitment of the leftist media varies. Leading the way, you have the most enthusiastic secular-progressives, the **New York Times** and other committed left-wing papers, but you also have legions of quieter S-P sympathizers. These mainstream media enablers provide aid and comfort for the frontline troops and are invaluable in getting their message out to an even wider audience.

Marching alongside the progressive print media are the Hollywood elite and a smattering of television people. They also help get the S-P message out and often marginalize the traditional opposition by mocking them or portraying them as wackos. Jon Stewart is a good example of someone who is not nutty left but who is clearly sympathetic to the S-P cause and who uses his nightly forum to promote it (admittedly, with a great sense of humor).

While some Hollywood people like Barbra Streisand and George Clooney are truly progressive fanatics, most of the liberal media figures are not in that category. They are more interested in themselves, in their personal success, than in some political jihad. However, they do enable the secular-progressives by failing to challenge their radical agenda while marginalizing any meaningful opposition that tries to block the road.

The ACLU, on the front lines, is extremely aggressive and well funded, as I have stated. That means they are serious people. On my programs, I have called this crew a "fascist organization" because they seek to **impose** their worldview on America—not by the popular vote, which is the way it is supposed to be done in a democracy, but by "gaming" the legal system. Because they know that they will never, ever achieve their goals on Election Day, their strategy is to rely on activist left-wing judges to bring about secular changes in our laws.

The most notorious example of this strategy is the gay-marriage ruling in Massachusetts. The ACLU helpfully pointed out to the Supreme Court of the Commonwealth that the state constitution had an apparent loophole: That is, the document failed to define marriage specifically as between one man and one woman. Presto! With the stroke of a pen, the liberal court wiped out more than three hundred years of legal traditional marriage going back to the founding of the Massachusetts Bay Colony. The ACLU was in ecstasy.

To this culture warrior, gay marriage is not a vital issue. I don't believe the republic will collapse if Larry marries Brendan. However, it is clear that most Americans want heterosexual marriage to maintain its special place in American society. And as long as gays are not penalized in the civil arena, I think the folks should make the call at the ballot box. Traditional marriage is widely seen as a societal stabilizer, and I believe that is true.

But if you are trying to secularize American society, gay marriage is a good place to start—thus the ACLU's fervor on this issue.

By the way, it is worth noting that Massachusetts is home ground for the ACLU. It is in this state where that organization volunteered to represent the North American Man-Boy Love Association (NAMBLA) **pro bono** in a civil case after a particularly brutal and (you would think) indefensible crime in Cambridge. I'll give you more details in the chapter on protecting children, but, briefly, a ten-year-old boy named Jeffrey Curley was raped and murdered by two men, who were caught and convicted. One of the killers had written in his diary that NAMBLA literature, which encourages adult rape of children, gave him some incentive to assault the boy. The killer has said he gained access to the NAMBLA material at the Boston Public Library. It was easy enough. He simply went there and punched up NAMBLA's Web site on a library computer.

Outraged as well as brokenhearted, the Curley family sought to avenge their young son and prevent any further heinous crimes by filing a $200 million federal lawsuit against NAMBLA. That gave the ACLU another chance to do what it often does: defend and promote harmful conduct based on a theoretical argument that any kind of censorship is bad. Think about it. What if Jeffrey Curley had been your child? Can you imagine the suffering and horror this boy had to undergo? And here comes the ACLU, guns blazing, ready to defend free of charge an organization that promotes the rape of children.

Too harsh? Not in my view. I have given you the no-spin truth. This is why I am fighting this culture war. This is why there is such conflict in America. Don't forget Jeffrey Curley—he is one of the main reasons the secular-progressives must be defeated. I truly believe the ACLU and its supporters are extremely dangerous. If these people win the culture war, the United States as we have known it for 230 years will cease to exist. This is the crux of the culture war: saving traditional America from those who want to change the country drastically—not by popular vote, but by judicial fiat.

I guess I have always been a traditionalist. As a history major at Marist College in Poughkeepsie, New York, I admired how the Founding Fathers crafted a Constitution that allowed individual achievement to be protected and rewarded. I saw the United States then, and now, as a generous, brave country that has liberated millions of human beings all over the world from tyranny. I admired the discipline and energy of a country that, in a relatively short period of time by historical standards, has become the strongest and most prosperous nation the world has ever seen.

But it has not been all good. There is no question that slavery and the systematic annihilation of Native American tribes are troubling, and each demands clear-eyed, honest introspection from those who love America. There is no excuse for either. If John Quincy Adams, who defended the rebelling slaves in the famous **Amistad** case, knew enslaving human beings for profit was an abomination, then Thomas Jefferson and George Washington should have known. And I believe they did. But the Virginians put their own economic security and comfort above justice. Washington owned more than three hundred slaves and they helped make him rich. Jefferson was also a slave owner, despite denouncing the institution as "the most unremitting despotism." Both Washington and Jefferson demonstrate the fallibility that every one of us carries.

The failings of America's great leaders mirror the failings of all human beings. All of us are sinners. But most sinners are also fundamentally good people, and so it is with America. It is a noble country, a place where 300 million citizens have more freedom than anywhere else in the world. Trust me. I've been to sixty countries; I know what I'm talking about.

So I believe we must strive to improve America, but we must also keep faith with the basic tenets of Judeo-Christian philosophy and competitive capitalism that the country was founded on. That's why I march under the banner of traditionalism. The brilliant men who forged the Constitution understood that Americans should have the opportunity to pursue happiness without government interference. They also believed for both moral and practical reasons that the greater good must always take precedence over individual selfishness.

Pursuant to that end, the Founders acknowledged that religion and spirituality could be effective bulwarks against anarchy and crime, so they encouraged a society "under God." But now all of that has been rejected by the secular-progressive movement, which holds that a widespread belief in a higher power is one of the causes of social injustice. In S-P land, "under God" is now "under legal review."

You would think the S-Ps would not have a prayer (sorry) of imposing their agenda on America. After all, the polls show that most Americans are traditionalists and the secular-progressives are heavily outnumbered. In fact, when polled, some 84 percent of Americans describe themselves as "Christians," and whenever things like gay marriage are put on the ballot, those things are voted down in even the most "progressive" states, like California and Oregon.

The frustration of the culture war is that the traditional army is largely on leave. Many Americans are disengaged from the conflict; in fact, they don't even know it's under way. Go to any shopping mall and ask people what they think of the secular-progressive movement and its impact on their lives. You'll likely get a blank stare followed by the inevitable "What?" But ask about the latest **American Idol** sensation and you'll have a detailed, open-ended conversation.

Now, I'm not being an arrogant wise guy here, because this is too important. Escapist entertainment has its place in a healthy life, but unless traditional Americans wake up and pay attention to important things like the culture war, they are going to arise some morning and find their old country has vanished—replaced by the politically correct utopia President Hernandez so kindly laid out for us in her stirring State of the Union speech.

And while the folks are otherwise occupied, one powerful and battle-ready brigade is very aware and actively engaged on the S-P side. That would be the aforementioned secular media—broadcast and print. The "image" aspect of the culture war is being furiously waged there. Unaware Americans are in real danger of believing all that they read and watch, and that would be disastrous.

Based on my thirty years of dealings with the national media, I believe the large majority of journalists sympathize with the S-Ps. Let me cite an example. That shrill, pitiful, and hateful far-left radio network Air America was welcomed at its debut with huge media attention—more than twenty positive articles in the **New York Times** alone. Of course, most of the press was deliriously supportive of AA. And it remained so even after Air America collapsed in the ratings and was involved in a dubious loan situation involving a children's charity in New York City.

It is fair to say that the print press **desperately** wanted Air America to succeed. Meanwhile, conservative talk radio **is** a huge success just about everywhere in the United States. How many newspaper articles have you seen about that? Chances are, none lately.

There is no question that the vast preponderance of America's newspapers have a liberal editorial philosophy. Papers like the **Boston Globe,** the **Washington Post,** the **Baltimore Sun,** the **Atlanta Journal-Constitution,** the **Miami Herald,** the **New Orleans Times-Picayune,** the **St. Louis Post-Dispatch,** the **Kansas City Star,** the **Minneapolis Star Tribune,** the **Houston Chronicle,** the **Denver Post,** the **Seattle Post-Intelligencer,** the **Oregonian,** the **San Francisco Chronicle,** the **Sacramento Bee,** the **Los Angeles Times,** and on and on and on. In fact, the only national paper with a conservative editorial page is the **Wall Street Journal.** Locally, liberal papers outnumber conservative sheets about ten to one.

Some newspapers, like the **St. Petersburg Times,** no longer even try to hide their secular slant. **Factor** viewers may remember how angry I was when Florida prosecutor Brad King refused to charge three individuals who helped the killer of nine-year-old Jessica Lunsford evade capture. King's action was as disgraceful a law-enforcement decision as I have ever seen. Little Jessica was brutally murdered by John Couey, who initially confessed to holding her captive for days in a small mobile home just yards from Jessica's house before suffocating the girl. Subsequently, Couey wrote me a letter stating that the others did help him evade police and, according to Couey, one of his "roommates" even knew Jessica was being held captive. But Brad King let the three go.

After I reported that terrible story and slammed King, the **St. Petersburg Times** attacked me personally. It is my opinion that the paper was totally in the tank for King, and its far-left editorial posture bled over onto its news pages. How dare O'Reilly make judgments about this case? He's just a conservative windbag. Let's get him. So they tried. To this day, I consider the **St. Petersburg Times** to be the nation's worst newspaper. There is no sense of fair play in the paper at all, and ideology slants its hard-news coverage. It's disgraceful.

If you still don't believe that the American media slants left-secular, then I'll try one more time to convince you. A media study based at UCLA and released in December 2005 concludes: "Almost all major media outlets tilt to the left."

The coauthor of the study, UCLA political science professor Tim Groseclose, summed up his study this way: "I suspected that many media outlets would tilt to the left, because surveys have shown that reporters tend to vote more Democrat than Republican. But I was surprised at just how pronounced the distinctions are."

The other coauthor, University of Missouri economist Jeffrey Milyo, was also blunt: "There is a quantifiable and significant bias in that nearly all [the media] lean to the left." The UCLA study identifies **The CBS Evening News**, the **New York Times**, and the **Los Angeles Times** as the most liberal news operations in the country (I know, you're shocked). Only Brit Hume's program on Fox News and the **Washington Times** were found to tilt right.

By the way, if you dispute the UCLA study, let me throw one more set of facts at you. In addition to being ultrasupportive of the secular-progressive movement, the **New York Times** uses its opinion pages to savage powerful people with whom it disagrees (almost always conservatives). And we're not talking polite debate here, either; we're talking "rip their throats out" verbiage.

The **Times** employs four columnists who utterly despise the Bush administration: Maureen

Dowd, Paul Krugman, Bob Herbert, and Frank Rich. In the year 2005 and the first two weeks of 2006, these individuals filed an astounding 149 columns lambasting the Bush administration; that was 47 percent of their entire work output. I mean, how much loathing do you need? The **Times** should just put up a daily headline on its op-ed page: "WE HATE BUSH." Why bother with the repetitive analysis? And remember, the **New York Times** is the Big Kahuna among the secular media; that paper sets the agenda for the S-P press.

So here's my conclusion based on the data: U.S. journalism is essentially in the grip of a pack mentality. Most media people are well educated and many come from affluent homes. Also, a good number are urban dwellers who see themselves as sophisticated gatekeepers of the common good. These people don't really have much in common with the "folks," but hey, everybody needs a guiding light to deliver them from the traditional darkness, right?

The split between "we" the people and the media is especially severe in the spiritual arena. A survey by the American Society of Newspaper Editors shows that the rate of atheism among journalists is about 20 percent, significantly higher than among the general population, where it stands at about 9 percent. When one in five media warriors does not believe in the existence of a supreme being, it's not hard to figure out why many press people support secular causes like unrestricted abortion, gay marriage, and restraints on public displays of faith.

This media "group-think" mentality is so powerful that even some establishment journalists are dismayed. Marie Arana, a **Washington Post** editor, was quoted in her own paper as saying: "The elephant in our newsroom is our narrowness. Too often, we wear liberalism on our sleeve and are intolerant of other lifestyles and opinions. . . . We're not very subtle about it at this paper. If you work here, you must be one of us. You must be liberal, **progressive** [my emphasis], a Democrat. I've been in communal gatherings at the **Post**, watching election returns, and have been flabbergasted to see my colleagues cheer unabashedly for the Democrats."

Asked for a reaction to Ms. Arana's comments, **Washington Post** editor in chief Leonard Downie replied that he was "concerned" if some staffers openly displayed political preferences. But Downie went on to say that his newspaper has "a diverse staff when it comes to ideological backgrounds."

Sure, and I'm Puff Daddy or whatever his name is this morning. Just imagine if a **Washington Post** reporter waltzed into the newsroom tomorrow and said: "Man, I love that **O'Reilly Factor**! What a great program!" That would do the guy's career a lot of good, don't you think?

Now, I know perfectly well that most Americans are not locked onto newspaper editorial pages—certainly not the way I am—but consider this: The same kind of group-think you have on the opinion pages is often on display throughout the rest of the paper. This is especially true among feature writers like book, movie, and TV critics. It is here where the culture war sappers do their finest work.

In his book **Hollywood Nation,** author James Hirsen did some terrific research. Going through America's largest newspapers, he compared the reviews for Michael Moore's movie **Fahrenheit 9/11** to those of Mel Gibson's film **The Passion of the Christ.**

Surprise. The critics, showing that group-think tendency again, loved Moore and hated Gibson. Here's a sample taken from Hirsen's book:

- the **New York Times**'s A. O. Scott called Moore a "credit to the Republic" but found that Gibson had "exploited" the death of Jesus.
- the **Washington Post**'s Ann Hornaday called **Fahrenheit** Moore's "finest artistic

moment." She criticized Gibson for bad history.

- the **Los Angeles Times**'s Kenneth Turan said Moore presented a "persuasive and unrelenting case." But Gibson's film was "inaccessible for all but the devout."
- And the **Boston Globe**'s Ty Burr urged readers to see Moore's movie but warned people that **The Passion** would leave them "battered and empty-handed."

Hirsen lists many other Gibson slams and Moore hurrahs to make his case that newspaper critics and feature writers are overwhelmingly liberal and many are committed secular-progressives. Why should you care what these people write? Because they can set trends, demonize projects they don't like, and define success in our popular culture. In other words, they have power. It is true that the folks have the final say (Gibson's **Passion** was an enormous success), but too many writers on popular culture are in the business of promoting the secular and damaging the traditional. No question.

The atmosphere has become so poisonous that I now rarely talk to the print press, and, as you know, I am a major blabbermouth. I've been burned time and time again by writers who took my words out of context and provided snide commentary leading into my quotes. Again, not whining—just reporting. Believe me; I have the clips to prove the case that pervasive secular bias is rampant in America's print press. Here's still more evidence, in case you are not believing me. (Is that even possible?)

The Tribune Company out of Chicago runs a chain of newspapers, primarily liberal, throughout the United States; papers like the **Los Angeles Times,** the **Chicago Tribune,** the **Baltimore Sun,** and **Newsday** on Long Island. Business at those papers, and many others in the United States, is not good. So the Tribune Company laid off almost one thousand workers.

That, of course, is a sad situation, but one group was particularly outraged. MoveOn, a far-left outfit dedicated to advancing the S-P cause and assassinating the characters of traditional Americans, presented Tribune CEO Dennis Fitzpatrick with a petition demanding that the cuts be stopped. MoveOn claimed the downsizing "undermined important watchdog journalism."

Sure. If you believe MoveOn cares about "watchdog journalism," you probably also believe George Clooney wants me as an overnight guest at his Italian villa. The fanatical S-P organization clearly knows that the newspapers run by the Tribune Company are a reliable S-P ally. Do you think MoveOn would petition against cuts on the **Wall Street Journal** editorial page? If so, you might also believe Howard Dean and I go camping together each summer in the Green Mountains. Bottom line: The more American newspapers decline, the worse things will be for the S-Ps, unless a miracle happens and newspapers become more fair and balanced.

In addition to the overwhelming liberal presence in print, TV comedians like David Letterman, Jay Leno, and the cast of **Saturday Night Live** all lean to the left, as do their stables of gag writers. If you think such people are not important to the culture wars, you've been in a coma for the past ten years. Huge percentages of Americans, including many people in their twenties, report that they get much of their "news" from TV comedians. That might sound like a joke, but it's absolutely true.

It's also true that on any given night, TV political humor is spread all around the ideological spectrum. But do the body counts: It's the conservatives who are mocked the most. The cumulative effect of print and TV commentary that largely denigrates conservative thought and traditional values cannot be overestimated. It builds up in the minds of many Americans. It becomes huge.

At this point, however, it is important to reiterate that the culture war is **not** between conservatives and liberals. Although it's true that most conservative Americans tend to be traditionalists, there are many people who hold liberal political views who are appalled at the goals and tactics of the secular-progressive movement. Perhaps the best example of this is Senator Joseph Lieberman of Connecticut, who, of course, ran for vice president on the Al Gore ticket (Gore is very S-P). Lieberman, and others like him, respect the nation's religious traditions and do not want radical changes in our established societal mores. They are liberal traditionalists. Another example would be Senator Evan Bayh of Indiana, a traditional guy who is also a committed Democrat.

It would be a big mistake, then, for conservative traditionalists to make enemies out of liberals who still see their country as a good and worthy enterprise. They should be welcomed into the fray. No, it is the people who see America as evil that traditionalists should be concerned about. It is the radicals who want a complete overhaul of American culture and law who are the targets of this book, not liberal thinkers. For example, I firmly believe John and Robert Kennedy would be traditional culture warriors if they were on the scene today. JFK wanted you to "do" for the country, while RFK was a staunch Catholic who had a blood feud with Castro. Ironically, the traditional posture of the Kennedy brothers might pit them against their youngest sibling, Teddy, one of America's biggest S-P enablers.

A good battle plan merits repetition. So, again, defining all liberals as secular-progressives is a huge tactical mistake. You see conservatives falling into this error every day, especially on talk radio. At this point, traditionalists of all stripes need to understand who the real enemy is and cultivate all the allies they can get.

American culture, in my opinion, has deteriorated drastically in large part because the ACLU, thanks to its enormous power, gets a free pass from most of the media. Many of the approximately four hundred thousand members of the ACLU are rabid in their support of the organization and are fanatically committed to the S-P cause. But there are a good number of other ACLUers who, I believe, have no idea of the group's true radicalism. They buy the smoke-screen propaganda and think the ACLU's primary mission is looking out for your civil liberties.

Well, let's examine the record.

Founded in 1920 by a man named Roger Baldwin, a dedicated secular zealot, the ACLU began as an openly radical group, quickly discovered that was a dangerous misstep, then took a strategic turn into "patriotism." According to author Peggy Lamson, a Baldwin biographer, he explained this strategy with chilling clarity: "I am for socialism, disarmament, and ultimately for abolishing the state itself as an instrument of violence and compulsion. I seek social ownership of property, the abolition of the propertied class, and sole control by those who produce wealth. Communism is the goal."

In the book **The ACLU vs. America,** by Alan Sears and Craig Osten, Baldwin's plan is also revealed unmistakably. The authors quote a letter he wrote to a supporter: "Do steer away from making it [the ACLU] look like a Socialist enterprise . . . we want to look like patriots in everything we do. We want to get a lot of flags, talk a good deal about the Constitution and what our forefathers wanted to make of this country, and to show that we are really for the folks . . ."

Eighty-nine years later, the ACLU is still using Baldwin's strategy, wrapping itself in the flag and defending the rights of the "folks." Unless, of course, the folks are Christians, Boy Scouts, parents who want to know if their underage daughters are having abortions, or concerned Americans who want sexual predators who hurt children held accountable. Those folks need not apply for ACLU membership.

The present-day ACLU is headed by Anthony Romero, a committed far-left culture warrior who formerly worked for the Ford Foundation, conveniently a great source of funding for radical left causes. (Started with funds contributed by Henry Ford and his son Edsel, the foundation is now independent of the Ford Motor Company or the Ford family.)

An openly gay activist, Romero has brought a ton of money to the ACLU by energizing wealthy radicals such as Peter Lewis and George Soros (more on him later). Romero is leading the charge to change the United States into a secular-progressive nation and is an effective and fanatical general for the S-P movement. He is a first-rate propagandist, unrelenting in his quest to bring down America's Judeo-Christian traditions. By the way, Romero has given orders to all his ACLU cohorts never to appear on **The O'Reilly Factor.** I must be the enemy! I take that as a great compliment, although Romero is welcome to come on the program anytime to set me straight.

Finally, in the first ten years of the Fox Newschannel's existence, I have succeeded in unmasking much of the ACLU's true agenda. Of course, not everyone agrees with me about the group, but I have their attention. In a letter to me dated December 23, 2002, ACLU media relations director Emily Whitfield wrote:

> Dear Mr. O'Reilly:
>
> I write to offer you sincere thanks on behalf of the American Civil Liberties Union. After your characterization of the ACLU as a "fascist" organization and your undefined call for "intense scrutiny" of the organization, we had the best day all year of on-line donations and new memberships . . .
>
> I'm sure this unintended consequence presents as much of a pleasant surprise to you as it does to us. Please keep up the good work.

I'll try, Ms. Whitfield. And the next time you see your Daddy Warbucks, George Soros, please tell him this: You can't put a price on the truth.

KEEP AMERICA
SAFE AND FREE
THE ACLU CAMPAIGN TO DEFEND THE CONSTITUTION

December 23, 2002

Bill O'Reilly
Fox News Channel
1211 Avenue of the Americas
New York, NY 10036

Dear Mr. O'Reilly:

I write to offer you sincere thanks on behalf of the American Civil Liberties Union. After your characterization of the ACLU as a "fascist" organization and your undefined call for "intense scrutiny" of the organization, we had the best day all year in terms of on-line donations and new memberships.

In fact, your campaign against us couldn't have come at a better time. It coincides exactly with our year-end giving season. If you continue your attacks, no doubt we will break long-standing membership and development records.

I'm sure this unintended consequence presents as much of a pleasant surprise to you as it does to us. Please, keep up the good work.

Yours truly,

Emily Whitfield
Media Relations Director
American Civil Liberties Union

A complimentary letter from my biggest fans.

Behind every effective political or social movement, there is a guiding philosopher to articulate theory and, sometimes, strategy. For communism it was Karl Marx. For democracy it was Thomas Jefferson and his contemporaries. And for secular-progressivism it is George Lakoff, a professor of cognitive science and linguistics at the University of California, Berkeley (the mother ship for S-P academia).

Chances are you've never heard of Lakoff himself; he is a shadowy guy. Although he's written several books and occasionally appears in far-left forums, mainly he guides radical left thought from his California perch and decries the horrors of "conservatism."

Lakoff's philosophy is easy enough to understand, and I'll define it by taking his own words from the book **Don't Think of an Elephant: Know Your Values and Frame the Debate:**

- "If you work hard; play by the rules; and serve your family, community, and nation, the nation should **provide** [my italics] a decent standard of living . . ."

You undoubtedly recognize this for what it is: standard-issue socialism, according to which the central government owes its compliant citizens economic prosperity. In other words, the government is there to **provide.**

- "Bring corporations under stakeholder control, not just stockholder control."

Again, another top ten hit from the socialism playlist: Control free enterprise by having a centralized government dictate what is in the public's interest and what is not. Fidel Castro loves this Lakoff guy.

- "It is the job of government to promote and, if possible, **provide** . . . more freedom, a better environment, broader prosperity, better health, greater fulfillment in life . . ."

There's that "provide" word again. I actually agree with this guy about more freedom and a better environment—who doesn't want those things? But then Lakoff goes off the rails, demanding "greater fulfillment in life." How nuts is that? Jimmy Carter's gonna come to my house when my roof leaks? Ronald Reagan owes me a pep talk if I'm depressed? Bill Clinton should act as a therapist for my screwed-up kid? George W. Bush should be clearing the brush from our yards?

George Lakoff, the Yoda of the secular-progressives.

Lakoff really believes

this nonsense. His vision is that first and foremost, a central government should make sure we all have fulfilling lives. Talk about a nanny state! No, this is worse, much worse—this is a **Dr. Phil state**!

Lakoff goes on to avow the following: Businesses should not adversely affect the public good; the United States should have a "values based foreign policy"; every American has a right to "state-of-the-art," affordable health care, and every child has the right to "high-quality early childhood education." Hold it. Doesn't every American deserve a masseuse, too? After all, how can we have fulfilling lives if our backs hurt?

What Lakoff absolutely wants to do is set up an enormous central government that **provides** (that word again) cradle-to-grave security and entitlements to 300 million people. And who would rule that central government? Well, people who think like George Lakoff, that's who; enlightened souls who can judge behavior and mandate social change in such a way that justice is perfect every time. In other words, Jesus would return to earth to run the United States. (Jesus the man—not the deity. Separation of church and state, you see.)

Herewith some other pearls of wisdom from George Lakoff, the Yoda of the S-P movement:

- "There is no such thing as a self made man." (All success is due to societal assistance.)
- "The United States has systematically promoted a terrorism of its own . . ."
- "In the 'nurturant' parent model, discipline arises not from painful physical punishment, but through the promotion of responsible behavior via empathetic connection . . ." (Translation: Lakoff would outlaw spanking.)
- "In the 'nurturant' form of religion, your spiritual experience has to do with your connection to other people and the world . . ." (This means the "higher power" concept is out; atheism is the way to go and would be subtly promoted by the government.)

Interestingly, the very far-left **Atlanta Journal-Constitution** is pushing Lakoff's central societal vision, that the "rich" owe everybody else, hard. On January 4, 2006, columnist Harris Green wrote: "Whatever the rich receive, it is not due entirely to their own talent and effort, as many would have us believe. They owe their parents. They owe the teachers and counselors and clergy who taught them and civilized them. They owe the farmers and truckers and grocery store workers who put food on their tables, and the firefighters and police officers and emergency medical technicians who protected them from harm and further harm. The list of people they owe is endless. Therefore, whatever success they achieve in life is due mostly to the talents and efforts of a legion of people."

This is standard-issue communist thought. The rich (affluent) owe everybody else, and therefore the government has a right to take assets from the rich (affluent) to pay the debt. The S-P movement will vehemently deny any sympathy with communist doctrine, but that is as big a lie as telling a successful person that the guy who sold him breakfast deserves part of his income that day. This secular-progressive belief in income redistribution and government seizure of private property is extremely important to keep in mind.

Finally, it's worth noting that Yoda Lakoff generally steers clear of issues involved with the abortion movement. I guess it's hard to find anything "nurturant" about that.

Now—and this may surprise you—I do not think George Lakoff is evil, or even devious. He is simply wrong, and history has proved that over and over again. There is no doubt in my mind that he and the S-P foot soldiers who follow him believe they own the high moral ground. In theory, you see, the S-P movement has it all: equality, humanism, generosity, and universal empathy. That's the theory. But in the real world, the S-P platform would be impossible to carry out because of one inconvenient natural impediment: human nature.

If greed, venality, fanaticism, sociopathy, sloth, and emotional illness did not exist, then the S-P vision might have a chance at success. But as we've seen throughout history, utopian philosophies are impossible to impose and totalitarianism is often the result of trying. Hello, Soviet Union, Cuba, and Maoist China.

Professor Lakoff is not some wide-eyed nut sending out Marxist propaganda on a low-rent Web site. He's a realist. He readily admits his S-P movement has so far failed to win over the hearts and minds of the majority of Americans. He blames this on the dishonest conservative movement that intimidates politicians, and on the sheer stupidity of the regular folks. But Lakoff advises his S-P soldiers never to say that in public. Instead, the radical professor issues the following dicta in his book to progressives who engage in public debate:

- "Never answer a question framed from your opponent's point of view . . . this may make you uncomfortable, since normal discourse styles require you to directly answer questions posed. That is a trap." (Now you know why I have instituted a "No Spin Zone" on my TV and radio programs—the S-Ps have been taught to dodge questions and recite rehearsed answers. I stop that cold, inspiring Lakoff's next offering.)

- "Stay away from setups. Fox News shows and other rabidly conservative shows try to put you in an impossible situation, where a conservative host sets the frame and insists on it. . . ." (That would be me, and the "impossible position" is that the S-Ps have to answer my direct questions or be labeled a dodger. That's okay on the ball field in Los Angeles, but death on a national talk program.)

My question is this: Why would Lakoff tell his acolytes not to answer direct questions, since, as he claims, they hold all the moral high ground? Well, the answer is simple: The secular-progressive movement is so radical and desires such a departure from American tradition that once the folks understand the implications of implementing the S-P agenda, rather than simply debating the utopian theory behind it, they will recoil. Therefore, stealth and subterfuge must be used by the S-P armies of the night if they are to have any chance of succeeding in altering the social landscape of the country.

I enjoyed reading Lakoff's book, because he is so honest on the page. He makes no pretenses. He wants a new America, free from the old traditions that he feels do not "nurture" the individual. The guy's a fanatic, no question, but at least he doesn't hide behind a façade.

Lakoff is godlike to the S-P faithful, and it's easy to understand why. He's a stealth warrior, a battlefield theorist of the first order. The committed S-Ps march to his drumbeat all day long. Howard Dean even wrote the introduction to the **Elephant** book. (Isn't it amazing how close Dean came to actually acquiring serious power in this country? In 2004, the S-Ps were sooooooo close.)

Anyway, I'd love to get Professor Lakoff on **The Factor,** but he's too wily for that. He knows I have his number and he knows the only media game in town that will expose his vision is the Fox Newschannel. So he avoids me and the network.

But he can't avoid this book.

Far more malevolent and powerful than George Lakoff will ever be is the moneyman of the secular-progressive movement, George Soros. Without this dangerous guy, Lakoff and his crew might as well spit into the wind. Soros is El Jefe of the S-P forces, a man whose vast fortune is directed toward undermining traditional America and replacing it with a so-called Open Society. George Soros is the puppet master, the man with the plan, a ferociously far-left force about whom most Americans know little or nothing.

Born George Schwartz to a Jewish family in Hungary in 1930, Soros assumed the identity of a gentile boy when the Nazis invaded at the start of World War II. Young George survived the Germans but fled Hungary when the Russians occupied the country after the surrender of the Third Reich.

George Soros, S-P jefe, puppet master, and moneyman.

Soros wound up in London, studied at the London School of Economics, then migrated to America in 1956, where he began an investment fund that eventually made him one of the richest men in the world. **Forbes** magazine estimates his personal wealth at more than $7 billion. Along the moneymaking trail, Soros was convicted of insider trading in France in 1988, earning a $2 million fine. He has gained a reputation as a ruthless currency trader who often dances on the edge of illegality. In 1992, he made $1 billion in a single day by betting that England would devalue the national currency.

Now an American citizen, Soros keeps much of his vast fortune in banks on the Dutch island of Curaçao, where his Quantum Fund is registered. That means Soros can dodge many U.S. corporate taxes even though he himself is based in New York City. By the way, George Soros is on record as wanting affluent Americans to pay higher taxes, even as he operates a lucrative real estate company from Bermuda—another place where he can avoid U.S. taxes.

What kind of man is Soros? Well, he does not believe in God, his social philosophy is libertarian, and his political outlook is far, far left. According to investigative reporter Peter Schweizer, a fellow at the Hoover Institution, Soros has donated "hundreds of millions of dollars" to American left-wing causes. At this point, he is the prime financier of a number of operations on the

Internet that consistently smear conservative and traditional Americans.

Up until the attacks on 9/11, Soros was just another ideologue screaming for legalized drugs (Joseph Califano calls him "the Daddy Warbucks of drug legalization"), euthanasia, and "progressive" taxation. But after the Al Qaeda attack, Soros became even more radicalized and more motivated. Through his Open Society Institute, which operates in at least fifty countries, he began funneling millions to groups opposed to America's war on terror and especially to those who criticized President Bush. According to the Center for Public Integrity, Soros spent $24 million trying to defeat Bush in 2004.

But most disturbing are his statements about the terror war and his support for a convicted terrorist enabler, New York attorney Lynne Stewart, who is currently in prison. More on her in a bit. Soros wrote the following words in the **Atlantic Monthly**: "Hijacking fully fueled airliners and using them as suicide bombs was an audacious idea, and its execution could not have been more spectacular."

Yeah, so what? The billionaire followed up that observation by taking out an ad in the **Wall Street Journal** that stated: "The war on terror as we have waged it since 9/11 has done more harm than good."

To whom? Whom exactly is Soros pulling for? It isn't the United States, as he has compared the Bush administration to the Third Reich, according to an article written by Laura Blumenfeld in the **Washington Post.** And in a **New Yorker** magazine profile he opined that the statements then–attorney general John Ashcroft made after 9/11 reminded him of how Nazi propagandist Joseph Goebbels jazzed up the German people's hatreds and insecurities before World War II.

Soros expanded on his post-9/11 angst in an interview with **Fortune** magazine: "The crisis now is the crisis of global capitalism and a political and military crisis. It has been brought about by the exploitation of September 11th by the Bush administration to pursue its policy of dominating the world in the guise of fighting terrorism."

In no-spin words, George Soros believes that the United States does not have the right to act unilaterally to fight terrorism, although, to be fair, he did not object to the removal of the Taliban in Afghanistan. A significant hallmark of the S-P movement, by the way, is that, with rare exceptions, a world consensus is needed in order to use military force. (Thank you, President Hernandez.) This, of course, is off-the-charts dangerous, because much of the world despises America and is decidedly not looking out for us.

And if all this weren't disturbing enough, George Soros then took it a step further by actually helping an aforementioned terrorist enabler. On February 10, 2005, radical New York City lawyer Lynne Stewart was convicted of conspiracy, providing material support to terrorists, defrauding the United States, and making false statements.

A jury found that Ms. Stewart had smuggled messages from her jailed client—Sheik Omar Abdel Rahman—to his Islamic terrorist supporters in Egypt. As you may remember, Rahman is the blind Muslim cleric who was convicted of plotting to blow up the United Nations and planning the first bombing of the World Trade Center, among other things. He had also urged his followers to kill all Jews. Rahman is serving a life sentence in a federal prison in Colorado.

Anyway, the sixty-six-year-old Stewart, who had openly advocated violence in the past, is now a convicted felon essentially for helping her pal Rahman. And guess who paid some of her legal bills: George Soros's Open Society Institute. Nice. One footnote: Both Soros and Stewart come from Jewish backgrounds, which is peculiar in light of their support for radical Islamists who want to re-create the Holocaust.

Continuing to operate pretty much under the radar, Soros has cemented his alliance with another billionaire, seventy-year-old Peter Lewis, chairman of the Progressive Insurance Corporation. These guys are working feverishly to ensure that the secular-progressive battalions are supplied with plenty of resources and firepower by which to pursue their global foreign-policy strategy and radical domestic agenda. Their primary attack vehicle is the far-left Web site MoveOn.org, which routinely slanders and smears perceived opposition. With MoveOn as a conduit, Soros and Lewis funnel money to other smear Web sites that target individuals in the media and politics for personal attacks. This is a nasty, nasty business and one that is constantly "evolving."

Peter Lewis, another major funder of S-P causes.

Even with the MoveOn hatchet machine in good fighting trim, both Soros and Lewis realize that they must reach beyond the Internet to move the S-P movement ahead, so they have mustered various elite media people to carry their water. Aforementioned **New York Times** columnists Frank Rich, Paul Krugman, Maureen Dowd, and Bob Herbert have all referenced far-left Web site postings in complimentary terms in their articles. Harvard pundit Alan Dershowitz used Internet smear material in a Los Angeles debate. **New York Daily News** entertainment columnist Jack Matthews and the paper's vicious gossip writers routinely use smear items fed to them by radical-left guttersnipes. **Dallas Morning News** columnist Macarena Hernandez and **Denver Post** columnist Cindy Rodriguez used information from Web sites under their bylines (Ms. Rodriguez was subsequently embarrassed by corrections printed by her employer). In fact, the far-left Internet smear merchants have solid access to the so-called elite media, something the far-right Internet bloggers will never have.

And these Internet guttersnipes will turn on their own in a heartbeat, as **Washington Post** ombudsman Deborah Howell found out in January 2006. Ms. Howell made the mistake of pointing out that indicted lobbyist Jack Abramoff funneled money to Democrats as well as Republicans. Even though that is true according to prosecutors, the far-left smear merchants organized a personal attack campaign against Ms. Howell. The result: The **Post** had to shut down its Web site after Howell was inundated with obscene threats. George Soros must be very proud.

But give S-P general Soros some credit for strategy. In just a few short years, he has developed a defamation pipeline that can instantly injure anyone in the United States. He has also used organizations like the NAACP and, ironically, the Anti-Defamation League to do his bidding, as both organizations have used quotes from far-left Web sites he has funded.

To sum up, Soros is a smart, ruthless ideologue who will stop at nothing to advance the secular-progressive offensive. He has no scruples, ethics, or sense of fair play. The guy reminds me of Colonel Banastre "Butcher" Tarleton, the most justly hated Redcoat during the Revolutionary War. Soros and Tarleton can both be associated with take-no-prisoner policies: In both cases, their prey, whether traditionalists today or colonial rebel fighters in the eighteenth century, were simply people trying to strengthen their country.

I mean it. For traditional-minded Americans, George Soros is public enemy number one. Without his unlimited cash (along with that of Peter Lewis), the S-P movement could not attack so readily and so effectively—and with such venom. Soros envisions a libertine society that soaks the rich (except for him) and forms no judgments on personal behavior. His one-world philosophy would obliterate the uniqueness of America and downsize its superpower status. His secular approach would drastically diminish Judeo-Christian philosophy in America and encourage his own spiritual philosophy: atheism. George Soros is truly an imposing force, and his elite media allies are making him even more so. We ignore him at our peril.

Two

Enablers at the Top

He who controls the air is likely to win the battle.

—**THE ART OF CULTURE WAR,** O'REILLY TZU

Most politicians in America, with the obvious exception of the President, hold only casual power; that is, they can make small changes and minor contributions to the country in their various capacities. The media hold the ultimate power to persuade. Without control of the mass media, the secular-progressives will never achieve power in this country, because, as I've mentioned earlier, most Americans are traditionalists and don't want drastic change.

But guess what? The mass media are not "most Americans." They consider themselves smarter than the average bear (that's you) and are tilting toward the S-P agenda more than ever before. The battle over

Christmas in 2005 was the most illuminating example of this; we'll deal with that incredible controversy shortly.

Over the past ten years, I have fought scores of battles against my peers in the media, and, as mentioned, I put their support of the S-P agenda at about 75 percent. My analytical conclusion was reached the hard way—I have been hammered each time I put forth a traditional point of view or championed a traditional cause.

For the past thirty years, television news has been dominated by left-leaning individuals who gave the S-P leadership hope. If the TV big shots sympathized with liberal causes, the S-P generals rightly reasoned, then the door was ajar for a more radical message, but that message had to be marketed with a delicate touch. Full-blown radical thought along the lines of Noam Chomsky, for example, would be impossible to place on the TV news. No, small doses of secular-progressive philosophy would be presented under the guise of liberal politics, and gradually the nation would be more open to things like gay marriage and legalized drugs. The strategy has worked very nicely, indeed.

Just for fun and insight, let's profile some of America's most powerful electronic media people vis-à-vis the culture war. As the title of this chapter says, some of these are the "enablers at the top"—people whose S-P proclivities set the tone and agenda for their powerful news organizations. I will analyze only people I know personally. We begin at the very top—the network anchors.

Dan Rather: A lifelong Democrat, Mr. Rather is an emotional reporter who often does not even attempt to hide his feelings. He lost his job on **The CBS Evening News** because of the President Bush/National Guard fiasco. You could not have missed this debacle, but most of the public read the situation wrong. True, Rather too eagerly smelled a huge story and has little use for George W. Bush, but he did not intentionally put a fake report on the air, as alleged in many conservative precincts. Instead, Rather left the micro work to his producer, Mary Mapes, who, in the end, could not authenticate key documents essential to proving the main point: that President Bush had used connections to avoid going to Vietnam in the sixties. As you know, Mapes was fired over the botched story, Rather demoted. Sad, but a fair outcome, because the stakes on that story were so high. It could have tilted the presidential election.

Some believe what happened to Dan Rather was his karma. I can't argue with that. Rather did have it in for the committed right wing in this country much more so than he did for the committed left. I believe he thought he tried to be fair, but his emotions and the liberal culture he worked in often overrode that effort.

Dan Rather's S-P leanings overrode his basic instincts for impartial reporting.

Here's some personal backup for that opinion. As a young correspondent working for CBS News in the early eighties, I put together a tough report on the summer homosexual invasion of Provincetown, Massachusetts.

Every weekend in the season, thousands of gays would descend on this small Cape Cod town, which was originally a Portuguese-American fishing village. While most of the gay visitors behaved themselves, some partied very publicly and explicitly. My crew filmed some pretty shocking stuff in the streets, and then we interviewed people in both camps. Predictably, most Provincetown officials back then were outraged at the sexual carnival, while gay leaders defensively chalked it up to a few idiots. Besides, they said, don't heterosexuals exhibit similar behavior on spring break?

My report was fair and balanced, but the footage of gay misbehavior was disturbing even though we blurred it on the TV screen. Dan Rather and his executive producer, Howard Stringer (now CEO at Sony), watched the piece, then promptly killed it. One of their minions told me it was too explosive and Rather and Stringer simply did not want the heat they anticipated from gay activists. End of story, literally.

I believe, though I could be wrong, that if some conservatives had been caught misbehaving on camera the story would have run. Or if gays had been the ones imposed upon, the story would have aired. But the Rather crew did not want to scrutinize the behavior of a highly vocal minority group. This is the kind of tilt that has been going on at CBS News for decades. The operation leans left, no question, and the aforementioned UCLA study backs that up. In the past, CBS News has been far more ready to promote a secular cause than a traditional one, and as managing editor, Dan Rather had a strong hand in shaping that situation. Maybe the new management at CBS News will change that culture; however, the hiring of Katie Couric to take Rather's place on the **Evening News** anchor desk is an interesting choice.

Ms. Couric is a decidedly liberal thinker. I've been interviewed by her a couple of times on the **Today** show and there's no question that her sympathies lie on the left. How dedicated she is to any agenda is hard to tell. Ms. Couric has broad audience appeal, and I believe CBS would have hired her even if she were a conservative, because her talent can translate into ratings. It will be fascinating to see if traditionalists get a fair shot on her broadcast. It will be to Ms. Couric's credit if they do.

The late Peter Jennings: For some reason, Peter liked me while many at ABC News, where I worked in the mid-eighties, did not. Like Dan Rather, Jennings was a tough, hardworking reporter, but he was far more interested in foreign news than the culture war in the United States. I think it pretty much bored him to tears.

Although Peter surrounded himself with liberals, he did have friendships with people like the conservative writer John Leo. Above all, Jennings liked feisty, challenging individuals. Despite what some conservatives believe, he was in no way an ideologue.

The late Peter Jennings.

In his private life, Peter Jennings was politically correct and probably favored Democrats most of the time. But I never saw Peter Jennings shade a story toward the S-P cause or denigrate a conservative for a point of view. I spoke with the man regularly. He did have a traditional streak in him, but largely kept it to himself. Jennings often watched **The Factor** and was greatly amused by the battles we fought—constantly telling me that I was completely insane to take on the elite media. But he was always supportive of me both publicly and privately, and he didn't have to be—there was nothing in it for him. Jennings may have been a bit too patrician for the hard right (some took it as condescension), but to me he was a straight shooter to the end, advancing neither secularism nor traditionalism on the air.

Tom Brokaw: I know him but have never worked with him. Still, I consider Brokaw the most liberal of the three network titans (this may surprise Dan Rather). His remarks to the press about the Fox Newschannel have bordered on the snide, and I resent it. For years, NBC News stopped just short of declaring itself a fellow traveler of the left. To be fair, Brokaw never crossed the ideological Rubicon, but he often went out of his way to read copy that was shaded progressive. He had full editing power and could have been more neutral.

Having retired from daily broadcasting, Brokaw is now a man-about-town in New York City and

Tom Brokaw, the most liberal of the network titans, in unaccustomed company: with me and Fox Newschannel boss Roger Ailes.

his social set is primarily liberal. I don't consider him a committed culture warrior, but I do believe his heart is with the progressives. I could be wrong, but don't bet on it. In March 2005, secular-progressive columnist Maureen Dowd of the **New York Times** actually floated Brokaw's name as a possible Democrat presidential candidate. That wouldn't automatically make him an S-P officer, but it does give you an indication of where he lives politically. Ms. Dowd is not going to become your champion unless you have solid S-P credentials.

Ted Koppel: A straight shooter, but you don't know where his gun is holstered. Plays it close on ideology and seems to dislike most of those holding power; in other words, Ted's a bit of a cynic (not a bad thing when your job is to watch the powerful). Very smart and well read, Koppel is definitely not a culture warrior and probably couldn't care less who wins the fight. I've never seen Koppel allow himself to be used on the air, but one of his former producers, a guy named Rick Kaplan, is a fanatic leftist who would smear any with whom he disagrees in a heartbeat. I know; I worked with Kaplan at ABC. How Koppel could work with an individual of this low character is one of the great media mysteries. I respect Koppel but could never really trust his fairness because of the Kaplan factor.

So based upon my assessment of these four network news legends, traditional Americans did not have much sympathy on their broadcasts over the past couple of decades. There is no Paul Harvey (who is traditional to the core) in network news. There's not even a Bill O'Reilly! Seriously, despite my success now, the networks never would have given me the chance that Fox News gave me. Never would have happened.

As for the other new blood on the evening broadcasts, I can't really evaluate them with any accuracy. All of them are highly skilled and none of them strikes me as engaged in the culture war to any great extent. So I've got nothing to report right now on these people. But their potential influence has been greatly diminished anyway; these days, what they put out to the public has little or no impact. Things have really changed since Walter Cronkite, a man whom traditional Americans once embraced on a massive scale. But Cronkite was really the conjurer behind a curtain. Unbeknownst to most of his viewers, he gave the secular-progressive movement some major growing room.

Walter Cronkite: He was not what he appeared to be on the air in the 1960s and '70s.

If you really want to know the prevailing attitude of those in control of network news, listen to Uncle Walter today. He has exploded out of the closet as a full-tilt leftist, complete with harsh remarks about conservatives and a proudly "internationalist" point of view. In the interest of full disclosure, I do have a dog in this fight. Cronkite hates me. I wrote a column calling him out on his opinion that other nations should have some say over how the United States defends itself. Walter took serious umbrage. (Come to think of it, there's a

Walter Cronkite, in happier days at CBS News with me and my Connecticut coanchor Don Lark. For years the most powerful man in broadcast news, he's come out of the closet as a full-tilt leftist.

lot of umbrage coming my way.) He told **Texas Monthly:** "O'Reilly said I was an internationalist! My God, what a terrible thing to be. I try to avoid his program whenever possible." No problem there, Walter, but being an internationalist when foreign terrorists are looking to kill us may not be the wisest thing.

Anyway, for more than two decades, Walter Cronkite was the most powerful media person in the world. And he ran a low-keyed, stealth-liberal operation. Walter was careful not to editorialize openly, but he had final say over which stories ran on the CBS News shows, how much time they got, and how they were introduced and edited for air. That's tremendous power, and I believe Cronkite used it to further his ideology in small but important ways. For example, he gave Democrat Lyndon Johnson far more leeway than Republican Richard Nixon. And he knew all about John Kennedy's "personal issues," his rampant adulteries and health problems and amphetamine use, but refused to report the story. Would he have been as accommodating to a conservative president?

Today, Uncle Walter is an openly enthusiastic liberal if not quite a secular-progressive warrior. He's more into politics than culture, although he has railed against opponents of gay marriage at the Commonwealth Club in San Francisco, and declared his opposition to the death penalty and his support of abortion.

Nearing ninety, Walter Cronkite no longer has to hide anything. As he was inaugurating a national newspaper column in June '03, he described his current viewpoint to the **Washington Post:** "I would call myself a liberal, but I hope I don't lose my ability to be dispassionate. My first [newspaper] column would be setting the record straight and pointing out what is a liberal and explaining why I think most reporters are liberals."

Well, with all due respect, I think Cronkite should have bestowed that observation on his viewers while he was sitting behind that powerful CBS News anchor desk. Goes to fairness, right, Walter? You could still have remained "dispassionate." By the way, Cronkite's newspaper column was a bust with the public and he quietly dropped it. I think many Americans were disappointed in him. Not that he's a confirmed liberal, but that he wasn't up front about it. Again, I could be wrong.

One last word about our pal Walter. In February 2005, a fund-raising letter went out from an organization called the Drug Policy Alliance, which advocates the legalization and/or decriminalization of narcotics. The letter was signed by Walter Cronkite. In the body of the cash pitch Uncle Walter stated: "We have locked up literally millions of people, disproportionately people of color, who have caused little or no harm to others."

What Cronkite is referring to is the 1990s crackdown on street drug dealers who sell hard narcotics to anyone with money, including children. Simple drug users are rarely sent to prison unless they commit another crime, like robbery, or violate their parole. But meth and heroin and cocaine dealers are sentenced to prison, as well they should be. Millions of lives have been ruined by drug dealers, and Walter Cronkite should be smart enough to realize that.

By the way, one of the big donors to the Drug Policy Alliance is George Soros. If you see him, tell him Walter Cronkite said hello.

Bill Moyers: Talk about confirmed liberals—this guy is the poster boy for the secular-progressive movement in the media. He actually did commentary for CBS News for a number of years. (And CBS wonders why conservatives dislike it? Come on.)

As the most visible face of PBS along with Jim Lehrer, Moyers has blossomed into an S-P bomb-thrower, perhaps the farthest-left broadcaster in the history of television. Few watched

Bill Moyers is the poster boy for the S-P movement in the media.

him before he left PBS (his average audience was about 1 million), but the guy lit it up for the S-Ps on his program **Now,** relentlessly attacking the right and cheerleading the progressive movement.

The thing about Moyers is that, unlike Cronkite, he won't admit he's a far-left kind of guy. But in the aforementioned **New Yorker** magazine article on George Soros, the S-P banker told writer Jane Mayer that he occasionally gets political advice from Moyers (as well as from Harold Ickes, the Clinton confidant). There is no question that Moyers is a hardened secular-progressive who is almost fanatical in his leanings.

Besides watching a few of his well-done documentaries about working Americans, I had never paid too much attention to Moyers until he started to attack me and the Fox Newschannel. I assumed his PBS program was a secular forum; after all, it was on the Public Broadcasting System, which has been an S-P stronghold for years at taxpayers' expense.

But after Moyers threw some bombs my way, I began to research him. Behind his public image as a "journalist," Moyers runs a foundation that doles out fairly significant money to left-wing organizations like TomPaine.com, which was conveniently run by his son, John. TomPaine routinely attacks Republicans and warns that the United States is on the verge of becoming a totalitarian state. So, while the taxpayers were footing the bill for Bill to bloviate on PBS, he was funding liberal causes behind the scenes. Shouldn't PBS have made that public in the interest of fairness? Maybe we should ask Walter Cronkite.

I could list far-left "Moyerisms" all day long, but let me give you one very offensive observation Moyers made on **Now.** The date was February 28, 2003: "I put it on [he is referring to a flag lapel pin] to remind myself that not every patriot thinks we should do to the people of Baghdad what bin Laden did to us."

Yes, you read that right. Bill Moyers believes that removing Saddam Hussein and setting up a system where the Iraqi people actually have the opportunity to freely elect their leaders is akin to a sneak attack by terrorists that killed three thousand American civilians. This über-liberal icon draws a comparison between the butchery of Osama bin Laden and the coalition action. Even if you oppose the war in Iraq, you must find that comparison odious and inaccurate if you have any perspective at all. Bill Moyers is quite simply Michael Moore's older brother as far as ideological thought is concerned. He is a true believer and ardent supporter of the secular-progressive movement. But he's also a man who commands respect in elite media precincts, winning all kinds of prestigious awards.

I've tried many times to get Moyers on **The Factor** so I could expose his radical thinking, but he's read Lakoff's book and will not show up. He told a Utah newspaper on January 15, 2003: "[O'Reilly] asked me on his show and I declined for the simple reason that I do not believe journalism is about journalists attacking each other."

Well, that's nice. Bill wants to give peace a chance. Swell. Then Moyers does an interview with Charlie Rose on November 2, 2004, and says this about Sean Hannity: "I've never heard such vile bigotry and belligerence as I heard [on Sean's radio program]."

Call me crazy, but I believe that might qualify as an attack. No?

End zone on Moyers: He's a man who firmly believes in the S-P cause and has dedicated himself to advancing it. I just hope Elmo wasn't influenced by him when Moyers was patrolling the halls of PBS. If Elmo and his crew go S-P, I'm beyond depressed.

The Morning Anchors: The network morning programs have more influence than you might think, especially among American women. Having appeared on all three broadcasts, I'd say Meredith Vieira and Matt Lauer are the most liberal of the bunch, but truthfully, their primary goal is to entertain and they certainly don't want to tee people off with controversial comments. For that reason the culture war is largely absent from the morning chatfests, although liberal book authors are generally given an easier ride than conservatives. But traditional America is a key audience in the morning and any outright alienation of that audience would be ratings suicide. The true culture warriors tend to be creatures of the night, making full use of darkness to wage their stealth campaigns.

The Late-Night Guys: All the comedians holding court post–11 P.M. are liberal guys. Jon

Stewart heads up the ideological parade, followed by David Letterman and Jay Leno. Stewart, whom I like, has taken **The Daily Show** sharply left and gives progressive guests a nice opportunity to present themselves as reasonable and looking out for the folks. But Stewart usually greets conservative and traditional guests with skepticism. On my last appearance with him, he was annoyed with my boycott of France. I appealed for Americans not to buy French goods because Jacques Chirac and his pals do not provide much help in the war on terror. Stewart thought my boycott call was misguided.

The Late-Night Guys—Leno, Letterman, and Stewart.

My reply to him: "Did you miss 9/11?"

Because the entertainment industry is solidly S-P, far more progressives get booked on all entertainment programs than do traditional people. Nothing particularly wrong with that, as Robin Williams is far funnier than Jerry Falwell . . . but, again, it's "advantage" to the secular-progressives at the net.

David Letterman's sensibilities definitely lie on the left, but he'll skewer anyone. However, he does on occasion promote dishonest radicals like Al Franken and relishes denigrating traditionalists. I enjoy jousting with Dave, and in what is now a broadcast legend, I appeared with Letterman on January 3, 2006. As soon as he introduced me, we began sparring. First, it was over the Christmas controversy (more on that later). Dave said I made the entire thing up. I told him he was misguided and provided three quick examples of Christmas under siege. But when radical antiwar protester Cindy Sheehan's name came up, things really got heated:

> O'Reilly: "The soldiers and Marines are noble. They're not terrorists, and when people call them that, like Cindy Sheehan called the insurgents freedom fighters, we don't like that. It is a vitally important time in American history, and we should all take it very seriously and be careful with what we say."

Letterman: "Well, and you should be careful with what you say also. How can you possibly take exception with the motivation and the position of someone like Cindy Sheehan?"

O'Reilly: "Because I believe she's run by far-left elements in this country. I feel bad for the woman."

Letterman: "Have you lost family members in armed conflict?"

O'Reilly: "No, I have not."

Letterman: "Well, then you can hardly speak for her, can you?"

O'Reilly: "I'm not speaking for her. Let me ask you this question. This is important. Cindy Sheehan lost a son, a professional soldier in Iraq, correct? She has a right to grieve any way she wants, she has a right to say whatever she wants. But when she says to the public, that the insurgents and terrorists are freedom fighters, how do you think, David Letterman, that makes people who also lost loved ones, by these people blowing the hell out of them, feel?

What about their feelings, sir?"

The conversation continued in this contentious vein and exploded into this final confrontation:

> Letterman: "I'm very concerned about people like yourself who don't have nothing but endless sympathy for a woman like Cindy Sheehan. Honest to Christ."
>
> O'Reilly: "No way a terrorist who blows up women and children . . ."
>
> Letterman: "Do you have children?"
>
> O'Reilly: "Yes, I do. I have a son the same age as yours. And there's no way a terrorist who blows up women and children is gonna be called a freedom fighter on my program."

David Letterman then went on to say that 60 percent of what I say is "crap." But then he admitted he does not watch **The Factor.** The next day, millions of people were talking about the shootout. Everyone, it seemed, had a different take.

And that was great because, finally, the culture war was vividly displayed on late-night TV.

I hope you got to see the interview; it was an important moment on the culture battlefield. By the way, in yet another example of how the "elite" media handles itself, CNN and NBC News ran stories about my dustup with Dave. In their presentations, they aired his most provocative statements to me but cut out my retorts back to him. Nice.

Some of my friends thought I should be mad at Letterman for insulting me on the air. But I wasn't. I don't care what he thinks of me. He's entitled to his opinion, and I have confronted folks on my program in a similar manner, although I am always familiar with what they have done. I enjoyed the debate and told Dave so. But if you saw that display, you can no longer have any doubts that David Letterman is a passionate advocate for the left. I won't say he's an officer in the S-P corps, because I'm not sure of that. But he is certainly not part of the traditionalist cadre.

That Letterman debate could never have happened on Jay Leno's program, because Leno is pretty much in it for laughs and is rarely confrontational. His famous line "Politics is show business for ugly people" is hardly partisan. I like going on his program, because he's not trying to make you look like an ass. He wants a few chuckles and appreciates the fact that I play along and set him up to mock me. Here's an example that aired on **The Tonight Show** just before the Iraq war started. He began by suggesting that if I interviewed Saddam Hussein, an opportunity might open up:

Leno: "Would you kill Saddam Hussein? Here's a pen. You open it and blow everything up."

O'Reilly: "You mean I have to go, too?"

Leno: "There's got to be something in it for us." (Big laugh, and I have to admit the timing was great.)

Although mostly harmless entertainment, the cumulative effect of the late-night programs does have a political message: Liberals are smart and conservatives are dense. Johnny Carson, who was much more of a traditionalist than any TV host working today with the exception of Regis Philbin, ran a fairly evenhanded ideological ship. But, let's face it, the S-Ps have a huge advantage late night (and even on the daytime shows) in getting their message out.

Now let's take a closer look at the cable news networks.

CNN: This network, which has never had a traditionalist anchorperson with the possible exception of business guy Lou Dobbs, tilts way left. Again, it is not on an S-P jihad, since parent company Time Warner is not on board with extremism, but the prevailing wisdom at CNN is the Ted Turner liberal, politically correct template. That stance has, by the way, hurt the network badly in the marketplace, causing traditionalist viewers to flee to Fox News.

Remember, the polls say that traditional Americans outnumber progressives about two to one. And, from what I can determine, there is absolutely nothing going on at CNN that would appeal to traditional Americans. This is another venue where secular-progressives are given an easy time—and they take full advantage of it.

MSNBC: The audience for this news network is so low it doesn't matter what they do. For the record, there are a few traditional people on the air there, like Monica Crowley and Joe Scarborough. But this outfit is not a factor in the culture war or anything else. Quite simply, it is one of the largest failures in broadcast history and, generally, an awful place in almost every way.

So add it up and you can see that the dominating influence in TV news, on the chat shows, and in print is S-P by a big margin. This is the great hope of the secular-progressive forces: that they can use the media to further their cause and diminish their traditional opposition under the guise of news coverage and entertainment. The positive media spin the S-Ps get does, indeed, influence some Americans, especially young people who may not have a strong frame of reference. Of course, Hollywood also trumpets the S-P agenda. So traditionalists are really up against it in the media—with two huge exceptions: talk radio and Fox News, which we will analyze forthwith.

And, as you read the following pages, please keep this in mind: Even though there is no question the S-Ps hold a huge media lead over the traditional forces, the brutal attacks on the traditional media are unrelenting and unprecedented. The vitriol hurled at so-called conservative media people by others in the press is almost comical. The next time you see the adjective "conservative" put in front of my name or someone else's, simply ask this question: When was the last time you saw the adjective "liberal" used to describe a journalist or pundit? Good question, right? Here's another good question: The S-P philosophy frequently touts "openness." They want all voices to be heard, they love freedom of speech. The ACLU is the freedom-of-speech poster group, is it not?

But the truth is far, far different from the S-P rhetoric.

I'm going to give the "last word" in this chapter to ABC newsman John Stossel, a libertarian and an honest guy. Stossel is basically a fearless investigative reporter, and after publishing a book that debunked some liberal myths, like the baloney that massive educational spending means a better educational environment, he learned something very interesting about the left-wing media in the USA. Says Stossel in his book **Myths, Lies and Downright Stupidity:**

> When I wrote my last book, **Give Me a Break,** I assumed the high poobahs of the leftist media would be eager to debate my ideas, if only to demonstrate how foolish my argument was, or to discredit the reporting of their misguided colleague who "had gone over to the dark side," as one TV writer put it.
>
> I was wrong.
>
> The conservatives were eager to have me; I got to discuss my ideas with dozens of radio talk show hosts and the stars of the Fox Newschannel. They made **Give Me a Break** a best seller. But the liberal media—CNN, NPR, and **The New York Times**—basically held their noses and ignored me.

Where was the "open discussion" the liberals always praise?

Where indeed? John Stossel learned what I have been saying for years: Secular-progressives drive on a one-way street all the time. If you don't agree with them totally, you are the enemy. You are to be shunned or attacked, depending on your influence and effectiveness.

"Open Society," my petunia.

Three

The Forces of Tradition

> Our petitions have been slighted; our remonstrances have produced irrational violence and insult; our supplications have been disregarded; and we have been spurned.
>
> —PATRICK HENRY

On October 7, 1996, the Fox Newschannel went on the air with about 15 million potential cable-subscribing viewers out of a U.S. population of about 300 million. At the time, the prevailing (and smug) wisdom in broadcast circles was that FNC would die a gory death, much like the CBS cable channel Eye on America. CNN patriarch Ted Turner was quoted as saying that his network would "squash Fox News like a bug."

That squishing sound you hear is Turner's prediction underfoot.

Ted's prognostication turned out to haunt him, as Fox News now reaches more than 80 million American homes and consistently hammers CNN in the ratings. The reason is simple: FNC is far more interesting to watch and allows traditional points of view to be heard, something CNN rarely does. Even on big breaking news stories like hurricanes and terror bombings, when no point of view is necessary, Fox News dominates.

There is no question that FNC has a far more traditional feel than any other TV news network in America. Analysts like Sean Hannity, Brit Hume, David Asman, and John Gibson generally approach issues from the conservative side, but there are also balancing voices on the left, like Alan Colmes, Geraldo Rivera, Greta van Susteren, and Juan Williams.

And then there's me. While I am, perhaps, the strongest traditionalist voice on the FNC team, my perspective does not translate into conservative ideology. As anyone who watches **The Factor** knows, we scrutinize all the powerful all the time—no matter where their politics lie. For example, I have scorched the Bush administration for its failure to secure the borders, its apathy toward alternative energy and other environmental concerns, its mistakes in post-Saddam Iraq, and many other issues. As everyone in the nation's capital knows, there is no political cheerleading on **The Factor** . . . period. We are watchdogs, not lapdogs.

As for the liberal side, I defended John Kerry in the Swift Boat controversy, sided with the Florida judge in the Terri Schiavo mess, and told the hard right they had it wrong about Dan Rather: He did not intentionally put on a bogus story about President Bush's military record (see Chapter 2). As I stated, he simply did not apply good journalistic discipline to that story and paid an enormous price for his mistake.

Fact is, I could give you scores of examples of how **The Factor** is an independent broadcast, but why bother? Facts and truth never satisfy the secular-progressives. They want to kill us because we are very effective in unmasking their strategies and exposing their dangerous agenda. You see, our huge success means, among other things, no more "under the radar" for S-P actions. They know that we're watching every move they make. I'm the spy satellite they desperately want to shoot down.

The Factor—along with FNC in general—also gives the Bush administration a fair hearing, and that also sends the S-Ps into spasms of anger. If you don't hate the President, you are an enemy of the S-P movement. It is that simple.

Ask yourself this question: What would the United States be like without Fox News? Have we not changed the landscape of America? Since nearly every other TV news operation leans left or is passively neutral, who would give traditionalists a break if FNC were not on the scene? The answer is: No one. Traditionalists would be essentially shut out of national television exposure. The S-Ps would totally rule, as they did before 1996.

That is what drives the far left crazy about Fox News (almost a pun, but not quite). It stands between them and total domination on TV—at least in the news arena. Also, FNC's audience and influence are huge. So the S-Ps have used all their power to try to destroy Fox News.

In one disgusting case, frantic Hollywood liberals actually financed an anti-FNC propaganda film that was played all over the world. Left-wing outfits like the Canadian Broadcasting Corporation and the British Broadcasting Company couldn't get enough of the Fox News slasher flick. Actually, because of its over-the-top dishonesty, the movie was somewhat funny in a demented way. Joseph Goebbels would have loved it.

Of course, the S-P propagandists conveniently fail to mention that just as many liberal voices are heard on FNC as conservative voices. FNC says it is fair and balanced, and while the hard left rejects that description, millions of nonideological Americans believe it, which is why Fox News wins the cable news wars every single night.

At the same time, as I will explain, we've learned to be wary of certain types of guests. In the first few years of **The Factor,** I put nearly all the S-P's I could find on the air. But we had one bad experience after another. Some of these loons would participate in an interview and then accuse me in the print press of abusing them off camera when the interview was over. Some of them filibustered on the air, making a give-and-take conversation impossible. A few of them ran to left-wing journalists and smear Web sites, telling outright lies about what **Factor** producers had said to them in the pre-air interviews. (It is standard practice for a producer to interview a guest off the air to get a feeling about the guest's verbal energy, articulation level, and sense of passion. This prep avoids putting people on the air who might not speak well or are too nervous to focus on their points.)

It took me a while, but I wised up: The S-P fanatics were not in it for an intelligent discourse, they were in it to injure the broadcast. It is hard to imagine a more loathsome group. So now I use only responsible liberals like Lanny Davis, Mary Anne Marsh, and former senator Bob Kerrey, to name just a few. These are honest, articulate voices and make **The Factor** a much better broadcast.

Newsweek columnist Jonathan Alter is a good example of what the S-P fanatics continue to do whenever they can. A committed secularist who hates President Bush, Alter wrote a column where he stated that Bush **knew** he had committed a crime by allowing the National Security Agency to listen to some phone calls without a warrant. You read that right: Alter flat-out stated that Bush **knew** his NSA order was illegal but gave it anyway. The journalist did not explain how he **knew** that—and I wanted to know just **how** Alter **knew**, because presidential decision making is usually kept top secret. Can Jonathan Alter read minds? Enquiring minds want to know.

So I invited Alter on **The Radio Factor** to explain his column. As soon as the interview began, he started to filibuster, refusing to stop talking and failing to answer direct questions about his assertions. This behavior was a contrived ploy on his part (yes, I can read minds, especially minds as predictable as the one Alter possesses). In the end, while he was gasping for air, I forced Alter to admit he had no idea what President Bush was actually thinking. It was Alter's unstated **opinion** that Bush **knew** he broke the law. Oh.

Not only is it virtually impossible to have a reasonable conversation with an S-P fanatic (or any fanatic, for that matter), it is also boring, because they will never cede a point, no matter how persuasive the evidence. So I'm now siding with George Lakoff and echoing his message to the far-left zombies: Don't go on Fox News. Just say no all the time. Avoid that theater of the culture war. If you are incapable of having a give-and-take chat, unable to cede valid points, stay off **The Factor** and FNC completely. Go on MSNBC instead.

The emergence of Fox News as a force in America has set back the S-P movement years and cost them a ton of money. Even though George Soros, Peter Lewis, and others continue to pump cash into the Internet sewer in order to demonize Fox News and other effective opponents, it is money down the drain. Only secular nuts take those sites seriously; most Americans avoid them entirely. Fox News is on daily display all over the world 24/7, and that power blunts the S-P jihad big-time.

The only other media force arrayed in formation against the S-Ps is talk radio. But here politics rather than the culture war is the main attraction. Hard-right talk is very profitable in America, but generally it concentrates on demonizing Democrats and propping up Republicans. This kind of chatter-clutter is soothing harmony to the conservative choir but doesn't really get into the fabric of the S-P war plan. While it's true that most Republican politicians reject secular-progressive thought, many Democrats do as well. As previously mentioned, we have to keep definitions and distinctions clear in the traditionalist armed forces.

In short, talk radio is not much of a threat to the S-Ps, because that movement is not concentrating on the ballot box right now. Instead, they are making their inroads through the courts and by brainwashing young, idealistic, and easily led Americans into believing that the secular vision is the way, the truth, and the light. The S-Ps lose virtually every ballot measure they propose (again, they even lost gay marriage in Oregon and California, big S-P states). No, for the purpose of the overall war, it is the judges and America's youth that the S-Ps plot to capture.

So right-wing talk radio doesn't have much effect on the deeper agenda of the secular-progressive movement. Some yakkers like Laura Ingraham have their number (as a former Supreme Court law clerk, she's seen the S-P guerrilla warfare firsthand), but most conservative radio people tend to bloviate about how good Bush is and how bad Hillary is, that kind of thing. Again, it's choir time. What the S-Ps fear the most is exposure, not endless ideological debate. They will lose the war if Americans figure out what they're up to. Talk radio usually does not provide that exposure, which is too bad.

The big positive on conservative talk radio is that it will latch on to the more outrageous aspects of the S-P jihad, like trying to knock the word "God" out of the Pledge of Allegiance, and the insidious attacks on Christmas. Because conservative talkers do blast obvious S-P excess, that movement does look for ways to hurt right-wing radio people, as Rush Limbaugh and Bill Bennett have found out. The larger Mr. Limbaugh's audience got, the more S-P criticism he received, some of it brutal. The glee the S-P press demonstrated about Mr. Limbaugh's drug saga was downright sadistic, in my opinion.

As for Bennett, in the summer of 2005, he got slaughtered for his metaphorical remarks on crime and abortion in black communities. His words were ripped out of context by a left-wing smear site and fed to mainstream journalists sympathetic to the S-Ps. The defamation pipeline swamped Bennett; George Soros and his pals had put another notch on their secular belts.

So adding it up, the traditional forces break down like this: Most regular Americans do not want drastic change in the country and therefore lean toward the traditional. A few of them actively oppose the secularists, but the mass of Americans are not yet enlisted in the culture war; they are a sleeping giant that, if awakened, could easily defeat the S-P opposition.

In the media, Fox News consistently provides valuable intelligence information in the culture war, and sometimes I'll step up and initiate an all-out battle (we'll discuss some of those in upcoming chapters). All in all, conservative talk radio can be mobilized in certain campaigns but, generally speaking, is preoccupied with partisan, elective politics, not the wider struggle between traditionalism and secularism.

As for the moneymen who support the right wing in America, these people are few but are worth mentioning in the culture struggle. Liberal think tanks have identified nine ultra-wealthy American families that, the left believes, have poured more than half a billion dollars into conservative causes since 1985.

Led by contributions from Pittsburgh businessman Richard Mellon Scaife, the right-wing money goes into conservative foundations and think tanks, and to groups that support issues like lower taxes, more restrictions on abortion, traditional marriage, and the Second Amendment (gun ownership). Next to Scaife, the Coors family in Colorado is the highest-profile conservative donor, but all of these families prefer to operate privately. There is no public bomb-thrower in the conservative donor community like George Soros.

It is hard to calibrate the influence of the conservative money. Certainly, it has helped elect Republicans and made it easier to combat referendums such as the ones on gay marriage. But, based on my investigation, it seems most of the right-wing cash is directed toward elective politics, as I've mentioned. Richard Mellon Scaife, for example, funded the notorious "Arkansas Project," which caused huge headaches for President Clinton. The Project was designed to dig up dirt on Mr. Clinton and feed it to the media. Much of the elite media rejected the information, but when it reached Matt Drudge and conservative guys like that, it quickly became public.

For traditionalists fighting the culture war, the far-right money actually damages the battle plan. The left can point to a variety of smear campaigns like the Arkansas Project and the Swift Boat attacks on John Kerry to justify their own attack machines. "If the right can do it, why can't we?" they wail. And there is some truth to that. But, again, the amount of smear exposure the far right is able to deliver pales against the defamation the far left can deliver because of elite media sympathies.

However, traditional warriors would be wise to avoid and, indeed, criticize personal attacks against the left that derive from conservatives. Taking and seizing the high ground is imperative in any military campaign and it is vital in the culture war. In addition to speaking out against the Swift Boaters, I criticized people trying to smear Ted Kennedy and anti–Iraq war congressman John Murtha. I also scolded Ann Coulter for writing that some left-leaning 9/11 widows were "enjoying" the aftermath of their husbands' deaths. That was way over the line, in my opinion. You can make your point without being mean-spirited.

For those stands, I took some heat from the far right, but my strategy is clear: If traditionalists want to win the culture war, they must fight with honor, because honor, as the true traditionalist understands, is a hallmark of America.

With that, the opposing armies have been defined. Now it's time to take a look at some victories and defeats on the culture-war battlefield, as well as some defining moments in that struggle.

Four

The Difference Between Us

To conquer a nation, destroy the values of its people.

—**THE ART OF CULTURE WAR,** O'REILLY TZU

As we've seen, there is a huge philosophical difference between secular-progressives and traditionalists, and that gulf will never narrow. Cultural détente is not in the offing.

Here's the basic divide: While most traditional Americans subscribe to the scriptural Ten Commandments brought down by Moses, the S-Ps have developed their own secular Ten Commandments. These edicts, as listed below, would have sent the Prophet screaming into the desert. Forget the golden calf; the S-P doctrine makes worshiping false idols look like midnight mass. Here follow the new secular-progressive commandments, handed down at Hollywood and Vine sometime in the late 1960s:

- Thou Shalt Not Make Any Judgment Regarding Most Private Personal Behavior. Man/Woman Is the Master/Mistress of the Universe and His/Her Gratification Is Paramount.
- Thou Shalt Not Worship or Acknowledge God in the Public Square, for Such an Exposition Could Be Offensive to Humankind.
- Thou Shalt Take from the Rich and Give to the Poor. No Private Property Is Sacrosanct.
- Thou Shalt Circumvent Mother and Father in Personal Issues Such as Abortion and Sex Education in Public Schools.
- Thou Shalt Kill if Necessary to Promote Individual Rights in Cases of Abortion and Euthanasia.
- Thou Shalt Be Allowed to Bear False Witness Against Thy Neighbor if That Person Stands Against Secular Humanism.
- Thou Shalt Not Wage Preemptive War in Any Circumstance.
- Thou Shalt Not Impede the Free Movement of Any Human Being on Earth. All Countries Should Be Welcoming Places Without Borders.
- Thou Shalt Not Prohibit Narcotics or Impede Personal Gratification in This Area.

- Thou Shalt Not Limit the Power of Government in Order to Provide "Prosperity" to All.

If you are willing to abide by those commandments, embrace and live them to the fullest, then the secular-progressive cause wants you. Bad.

I know, some of you may think I am exaggerating. Not so. Those secular commandments are all part of the current S-P political agenda. Look it up. And this libertine thinking is not limited to S-P cranks in Berkeley, California, or Boulder, Colorado. To prove my point, let's turn again to holy writ for the secular-progressive movement: the pages of the **New York Times.**

Every Sunday, a man named Randy Cohen writes a column in the paper's magazine called "The Ethicist." That's ethics as in "the principle of **right** conduct." On September 6, 2005, Mr. Cohen printed this question from an anonymous correspondent who lives in Brooklyn, New York: "I live in a gentrifying neighborhood. Someone on the block is dealing drugs that, I recently learned, are less benign than I'd assumed; he's dealing crystal meth. I believe the drug laws are overly punitive, and I've never had a problem with the dealer. But I would like to see the block cleaned up and the drug traffic gone. What's the morality of narcking on the neighbors?"

Thereupon, Randy Cohen, the ethicist at the **New York Times,** gave the following moral advice: "If your local drug dealer is merely unsightly, do nothing. This is not to endorse dealing crystal meth but to assert that the war on drugs does more harm than the drug use it seeks to suppress. I would be reluctant to invoke laws that can be both inflexible and ineffectual."

Cohen goes on to compare prosecuting American dope dealers to the eighteenth-century English courts that sentenced people to death for a variety of crimes that we would find today to be misdemeanors. His point, if you can believe it, was that good people should decide for themselves what laws should be obeyed.

This kind of blather would be comical if it were not so dangerous. Oh, by the way, speaking of comedy . . . exactly who is ethicist Randy Cohen? Well, he's a former gag writer for Rosie O'Donnell's daytime talk show and for **Late Night with David Letterman.** According to a friendly profile in the **New Jersey Jewish News,** Cohen has no background in theology, law, or philosophy. He's a gag writer! This is who the **New York Times** is trotting out as its primary adviser on right and wrong. Swell.

It is hard to believe, but Randy Cohen is basically telling his readers that prosecuting drug dealing is not a just cause, it is not morally **right**.

Never mind that hard drugs like crystal meth destroy thousands of human beings every year and also contribute to horrendous crimes like child abuse and violent adult confrontations. . . .

Never mind that meth users spread the AIDS virus through the sharing of infected needles. . . .

Never mind that drug dealing has caused catastrophic damage to the nation's poorest neighborhoods, often corrupting children and destroying families. . . .

Never mind that any person who would sell a substance as harmful as crystal meth (or any other hard drug) is a villain who deserves harsh punishment for peddling a substance that hurts so many human beings. . . .

Never mind all those things. The ethicist Randy Cohen, the man who defines what's **right** at the **New York Times**, doesn't like drug prohibitions, so he urges Americans to tolerate illegal drug dealing in their neighborhoods.

This, ladies and gentlemen, epitomizes the secular-progressive mind-set and the attitude of one of the nation's most widely read newspapers. This is exactly what the culture war is all about. What kind of country do you want? A country where a moral relativist like Randy Cohen defines right and wrong and dispenses ethical advice? A country where, if you don't like the law, you allow lawbreakers to run wild? Isn't that anarchy?

It is apparent to me that the **New York Times** has deteriorated into a secular-progressive training manual, encouraging its opinion writers to spew forth radical and often dishonest viewpoints that badly damage America. Yes, I know the United States is a great nation because of diversified opinion and robust debate, but under publisher Arthur Sulzberger III and editor Bill Keller, the **Times** has become the country's foremost promoter of secular-progressive lunacy. I mean, come on, allowing a guy who sells crystal meth to operate with impunity? What kind of nutty analysis is that? What kind of newspaper employs an **ethicist** whose definition of right and wrong is, basically, "Do whatever you want even if it encourages illegality"?

But the S-P agenda of the **New York Times** goes much deeper than just the writings of some loopy "ethicist." The paper's worldview is decidedly secular-progressive, and that spills over into just about every area. For example, in February 2006, a Danish newspaper published some political cartoons mocking the prophet Muhammad. The intent of the cartoons was to show the Islamic world that killing innocent people in the name of religion is insane. I'm sure you remember the controversy, as it caused a number of riots and deaths all over the world.

Anyway, the **New York Times** refused to print the cartoons, and I did not show them on my program, either. I actually agreed with the **Times** that the cartoons were insulting to Islam and the story could be reported without a demonstration of the cartoons.

But then, in a sidebar article explaining the power of visual images, the **Times** printed a picture of Mary, the mother of Jesus, covered with dung. That picture was taken at a disgraceful "art" exhibit in the Brooklyn Museum in 1999, which occasioned well-deserved controversy and outrage. So wasn't printing that image insulting to Christians? The paper declined to insult Islam but was more than willing to show an image that might offend Christians. What kind of an editorial decision is that?

Also, the **Times** had previously supported the exposition of a play called **Corpus Christi** that featured a gay, noncelibate Jesus. The paper called people objecting to the play enemies of "artistic expression."

So I'm sure you're getting the picture here: Insulting Christianity is freedom of expression and should be allowed, but mocking Islam is another matter. I'll explain the why behind the media anti-Christian bias later, when we examine the war against Christmas, but believe me, it has been going on for years in the S-P press.

The tragedy is that the **New York Times** has a bunch of brilliant people working for it. If there was anyone in charge with a lick of sane perspective, the paper could provide a powerful watchdog role that would greatly enhance the lives of Americans. Instead, the paper has become a gleeful purveyor of S-P propaganda and an attack vehicle against traditionalists. What a loss for America. It is beyond sad.

So count anti-Christian people and America's drug dealers among those delighted with the secular-progressive movement. As I've pointed out, George Soros and Peter Lewis, the S-P moneymen, are not real big on religion but are huge on drug legalization. Lewis was described as a "functioning pothead" in a **Fortune** magazine article and was arrested in New Zealand in 2000 on drug charges that were later dropped. Soros's big-money backing of medical marijuana legislation has led to chaos in San Francisco and parts of Oregon. With media like the **New York Times** providing a strong wind at their back, it is high times for Soros, Lewis, and also for their simpatico pal Randy Cohen. High times, indeed.

Five

The Battle for Christmas

> Happy, happy Christmas that can win us back to the delusions of our childish days, that can recall for the old man the pleasures of his youth, that can transport the sailor and the traveler, thousands of miles away, back to his own fireside and his quiet home.
>
> —CHARLES DICKENS

I think it's safe to say that Mr. Dickens would not have approved of the ACLU or the secular-progressive strategy to diminish Christmas in America. In fact, the perennially beloved English writer would have been shocked and appalled had he, in the year 1865, taken a time-machine ride forward to Christmastime 2005. But I also think ol' Charles would have liked me, and I **know** Tiny Tim would have.

Please trust me when I tell you that, just a few years ago, I never envisioned being a culture warrior on behalf of Christmas. To me, Christmas has always been the most magical time of the year. I remember as a small child sitting on the stairs early Christmas morning before anyone else was up, staring down at the scene before me. Santa Claus had come! All the presents were neatly wrapped and perfectly placed under the tree (a real one). I was mesmerized. What treasures would my sister and I be getting? I just sat there and soaked it all in. I remember the moments vividly. Why would **anyone** want to mess with Christmas?

But in recent years, the traditions of Christmas began to be portrayed in some quarters as somehow "controversial," which really teed me off. So, in the fall of '05, I set out to alert the nation that Christmas traditions were under siege and behind the action was a well-thought-out S-P campaign to marginalize the national holiday (which was almost unanimously approved by Congress and signed into law by President U. S. Grant on June 28, 1870).

Night after night on my TV program, I presented the evidence: Giant retailers like Sears (and others) had banned the mention of the word "Christmas" in seasonal advertising. The Lowe's Company told its store managers to sell "holiday" trees, not Christmas trees. The city of Boston changed the name of its Christmas tree on the Common to "Holiday Tree." (It was changed back after Mayor Thomas

Menino intervened.) There were scores of other examples.

But why? Why did the word "Christmas" suddenly become controversial? Why did I have to spend quality TV time on this issue and, above all, why was I so viciously attacked in the media for making the situation public? Let us now analyze those questions.

The ACLU began targeting Christmas at the start of the new millennium. Its anti-Christmas campaign began in small towns like Baldwin City, Kansas, where a local public school had a tradition of having an adult dressed as Santa Claus visit little elementary-school children, much to their delight. One year, a Protestant clergyman played the role of Saint Nick. That was it. The ACLU pounced, sending a letter to the school board demanding that **all** visits from Santa stop immediately because of the "religious" component.

The Baldwin City School Board fought back and won, thanks to attorneys from the Arizona-based Alliance Defense Fund, who often go **mano a mano** with the ACLU lawyers over anti-Christian litigation. The courts have ruled time after time that secular symbols of the Christmas holiday like Santa Claus are not illegal, nor are displays of religious symbols if other displays are permitted as well. But that does not stop the ACLU madness. You have to give it to them: These secular warriors are truly relentless.

The list of "controversies" got longer. In Benton, Louisiana, in Tipton, Iowa, in Cranston, Rhode Island, to name just a few places, the ACLU filed or threatened to file lawsuits objecting to Christmas displays. Each time, the ACLU lost.

Then the fanatical group turned its attention to trying to ban Christmas carols in public schools by threatening legal action against a school board in Elizabeth, Colorado. But the Tenth Circuit Court of Appeals, based in Denver, ruled that schools could permit traditional Christmas songs as long as students had an "opt-out" option.

So the ACLU lost again? No, because in reality the expense of fighting such lawsuits intimidated many school districts and city councils. Gradually, Christmas trees did become "holiday trees," Christmas vacation became "winter" vacation, and Christmas parades became "Festivals of Lights." The ACLU had won in the public arena, even though it lost in court.

Let me give you one final example that encapsulates the absurdity of this whole attack on Christmas. At the Ridgeway Elementary School in Dodgeville, Wisconsin, administrators allowed a play to be put on that featured the tune of the classic German Christmas carol "Silent

Night," but with a change in the lyrics. The Ridgeway version of "Silent Night"—which was written in 1818, by the way—went like this, if you care to hum along:

Cold in the night, no one in sight,
Winter winds whirl and bite.
How I wish I were happy and warm,
Safe with my family, out of the storm.

Is that unbelievable? I believe even Jesus would be shaking his head. How do you say "give me a break" in Aramaic?

So how have we arrived at this ridiculous point? The answer to that question is the semi-successful perversion of the U.S. Constitution. The ACLU and other secular-progressive groups constantly say they are challenging public displays of Christmas and other spiritual expositions to **protect** Americans from the emergence of a "theocratic" government—that is, a governmental system driven by religious thought and judgments. The tired "separation of church and state" argument is used again and again to justify attacks on spirituality in the public square.

But the "separation" argument is one big lie, a bogus piece of propaganda cooked up by an intentional misreading of the intent of the Constitution. This "wall of separation" falsehood has, however, been lovingly embraced by the secular media and foisted upon the American public with a ferocious intensity.

Perhaps the most precise analysis of the bogus separation of church and state argument was put forth by Senator John Cornyn of Texas, who wrote:

> For generations, Christmas trees, nativity scenes, Menorahs and other traditional public holiday items have been displayed in places of business and public squares, largely without objection. Groups could sing carols, schools could hold pageants, children could exchange Christmas cards . . .
>
> Today, however, it seems the first order of business every December may soon be for Americans to consult their lawyers. For only then might they know whether they are in the proper setting or sufficiently in compliance with complicated Supreme Court "multi-pronged" or "balancing" tests before celebrating [Christmas or Hanukah].
>
> The First Amendment clearly provides that Congress shall make no law respecting an establishment of religion nor interfering with the free exercise thereof. Nothing in

these provisions requires government to be hostile to religious speech or religious liberty. The Constitution nowhere requires government to expel expressions of faith from the public square nor forbids government from acknowledging—indeed celebrating—the important role faith plays in the lives of the American people.

Yet some courts, led by the U.S. Supreme Court, have demonstrated an unmistakable hostility toward religious expression in the public square. This effort to cleanse virtually all things religious from public life, including Christmas, is impossible to ignore and is contrary to our nation's founding principles.

Public expression of faith—one of the very freedoms most cherished by our Founding Fathers—should not be allowed to fall victim to a pervasive misunderstanding of the First Amendment perpetuated by a handful of secularists and judicial activists. In particular, during this time of religious celebration for so many Americans (Christmas and Hanukah), we should remember that we should, by right, be free to exercise our religious beliefs openly and to celebrate those beliefs as we choose.

Kudos to Senator Cornyn. President John Adams could not have said it better himself.

There is ample evidence that the Founding Fathers were exactly in tune with Senator Cornyn's analysis. While disagreeing with me about the Christmas controversy on my radio program, a caller adamantly claimed that founder James Madison was an "avowed atheist" who would have supported the S-P attack on Christmas. Of course, that's nonsense. I scolded the caller, pointing out that Madison, while not a particularly religious man along the lines of, say, John Adams, made numerous references to the benefits of spirituality in his public statements, including this one documented by the American Historical Association: "All men should enjoy the fullest toleration in the exercise of religion according to the dictates of conscience, unpunished and unrestrained by the magistrate."

Let's see . . . "unrestrained by the magistrate" . . . "full toleration" . . . I believe that means Madison would encourage all of us to say "Merry Christmas," including those working at Sears, where ol' James might be getting his tires and buggy whips.

While the religious aspect—Christianity—is certainly in the forefront of the Christmas controversy, the political agenda in the war on

Christmas has remained largely hidden. It is a decidedly covert operation, in other words. In fact, many people were surprised when I said on TV and radio that politics, not religion, was the driving force behind the attempt to keep Christmas behind closed doors.

Here's my explanation in a nutshell: Almost every social change the secular-progressive movement wants to achieve is opposed by religious Americans. Therefore, the more the S-Ps can diminish religious influence in America, the faster their agenda can become a reality. For example, the S-Ps are furious that gay marriage initiatives keep getting voted down, even in the most liberal states, and believe that the primary opposition comes from organized religion rallying their flocks to oppose homosexual nuptials with sin-based arguments. But gay marriage is just the start.

The S-Ps want no restrictions of any kind on abortion. That means they approve of partial-birth abortion up until the actual birthing process without a defined catastrophic health situation that could endanger the mother. In other words, the S-Ps believe a woman can end a pregnancy for any reason, at any time, under the banner of "reproductive rights." Some S-P loons even contend it should be legal to kill a baby up until the time the umbilical cord is detached. Obviously, most religions would find that blatantly sinful, to say the least.

On the same issue, secular-progressives want girls of any age to be able to obtain abortions without parental consent or even notification. Do you know of any traditional religion that endorses that extreme view? Even Henry VIII would be offended.

S-Ps are also behind the euthanasia movement, which is, again, opposed by many religions on the same grounds as abortion. A hallmark of most traditional theology is that only God has the right to decide the matters of birth and death.

Want another one? Legalized narcotics is frowned upon by many organized religions because intoxication is not considered a healthy act; that is, it does not bring a person closer to God—or to anyone else, for that matter. As previously stated, S-P bankers George Soros and Peter Lewis are pouring millions of dollars into campaigns to legalize drugs.

Organized religions also tend to oppose unbridled personal gratification and the idea that the individual is the center of the universe. In fact, on just about every moral topic, the S-P playbook and traditional Bible passages are at odds.

So, for the S-P agenda to succeed, religion in America must be deemphasized, just as it already has been in Western Europe and Canada, where secular-progressives have made huge gains. Looking at the entire battle zone, we can see that the American S-P generals have learned that goal number one is to secularize the American public school system in order to drive children away from religion and into the S-P camp. And what is the most wondrous display of religion worldwide? Why, Christmas, of course. Little kids seeing a manger display just might develop a curiosity about this baby Jesus person. What's this Christmas deal all about, anyway? There is no danger of that happening with winter solstice or with a holiday tree. Is there?

The secular-progressive press strongly disputes my analysis linking the attacks on Christmas to far-left, secular politics, but I stand by my hypothesis. I know politics is behind the war on Christmas because S-P philosopher George Lakoff told me so on page 102 of his **Elephant** book. There he urges liberal Christians to move away from Jesus to a broader "vision" of God and salvation:

> [The conservative] God is understood as punitive—that is if you sin you are going to

> hell, and if you don't sin you are going to be rewarded. Since people tend to sin at one point or another in their lives, how is it possible for them to ever get to heaven? The answer in conservative Christianity is Christ. What Jesus does is offer them a chance to get to heaven [if they toe the line].
>
> But liberal [S-P] Christianity is very, very different. Liberal Christianity sees God as essentially beneficent, as wanting to help people.

So what Lakoff is embracing is an S-P God putting forth the standard S-P doctrine of no judgments on most human behavior. Since the Gospels have Jesus [God] in the judgment business (and Him alone—remember the "cast the first stone" passage), the S-P movement must move away from the traditional view of Jesus. Thus, the less said, the better about anything to do with Him. So there you have the genesis (sorry) of the Christmas controversy.

Now, admittedly, this is heady stuff. I have thought long and hard about it. But it makes no sense to attack one of the most cherished traditions in America, Christmas, without a powerful ulterior motive. And Lakoff provides one. A God of judgment is not helpful to the secular-progressive cause; that is for certain.

Nothing if not pragmatic, the S-P brain trust knows a complicated explanation of liberal theology would be impossible for most Americans to even listen to, much less accept. So, using the diversity ruse, they have first attacked Christmas as being "divisive." How many times have you heard S-Ps say that the words "Merry Christmas" are offensive to many people? Well, that's another falsehood. According to a 2005 Gallup poll, only 3 percent of Americans say they are offended by hearing or seeing the words "Merry Christmas." And since we can assume that 3 percent of any population is certifiable—there is absolutely no problem in the United States with respect to "Merry Christmas." (By the way, pollsters always warn that the margin of error in a typical poll is also 3 percent or a similar number. Meaning, maybe everyone likes Christmas except the S-P leadership and a few media fanatics.)

It is hard to believe, but some CEOs of major retailers bought into the secular nonsense about Christmas and so they had to be educated. And they were. At the beginning of the 2005 Christmas season, outfits like Wal-Mart, Sears/Kmart, Costco, and Kohl's were hesitant to use the words "Merry Christmas" in their advertising. A few weeks later, however, **The Factor**'s reportage combined with a concentrated public outcry had convinced all of them that the greeting was appropriate and welcoming—and that, in fact, ignoring it was bad for business.

And so the great battle for Christmas 2005 was won by traditional forces, but not before there was a Battle of the Bulge–like offensive launched by the secular media. A charge that, as we will see, was ferocious in its intensity.

The No Spin truth is that I have never had a good relationship with the print press or even with many of my peers in the electronic media, as I noted in Chapter 2. I am cocky, outspoken, well paid, and critical of the mainstream American media in general. Over the years, only a few writers, like **TV Guide**'s Mark Lasswell and newspaper columnists Liz Smith, Cindy Adams, and Denis Hamill, have been complimentary of my work. The rest of the print press generally despises the overall "O'Reilly Factor" concept and, with a few exceptions, loathes me personally.

I . . . don't . . . care.

In fact, I loathe many of them right back, which, I admit, is immature. I sincerely feel that many of these newspaper people are jealous, mean-spirited, petty, and cowardly. For those reasons, I rarely speak to any of them. It took years, but I finally wised up: The print press is not looking out for me and never will be. Collectively speaking, they'd be happy if I got run over by a train.

Which, figuratively speaking, did happen in the war-on-Christmas controversy; the media came after me with a vengeance that reached ludicrous proportions. More than thirty separate newspapers attacked me by name for defending Christmas traditions. Not one media person that I'm aware of mentioned my name in a positive way. Not even Bill Moyers.

The plan of attack in the press was to charge that I "fabricated" the Christmas controversy to "get ratings." Yeah, that's the ticket. Never mind that lawsuits were flying and that a number of stores had eradicated any mention of Christmas in their advertising displays. No, according to the press, I made up the entire deal (and the evidence be damned). S-P sympathizer Sam Donaldson put it this way on the ABC News Sunday-morning show: "There's no war on Christmas. There's a Bill O'Reilly attempt [to get ratings]. Bill O'Reilly wants ratings. He wants to stroke the yahoos—where is Mencken when we need him—in his audience by saying there is a war on Christmas."

Somehow Donaldson missed the lawsuit against the city of Palm Beach, Florida, which allowed a menorah display but banished the Nativity scene. Palm Beach lost this one in court, and the city's taxpayers were out hundreds of thousands of dollars in legal fees. (By the way, Sam's reference to H. L. Mencken concerned a short book he wrote called **Christmas Story.** It's satirical but doesn't diss the concept of Christmas, just those who would spoil it with hypocrisy.)

While reading Mencken, Donaldson apparently also missed lawsuits filed by the ACLU against Christmas symbols in Rhode Island and Louisiana. The ACLU lost both times. But Sam wasn't the only one ignoring the evidence. My pal David Letterman, in addition to not liking my stance on Cindy Sheehan, didn't like my Christmas take either, as he made plain in our TV chat: "I don't think this [Christmas litigation] is an actual threat. I think it's something that happened here and there, and so people like you are trying to make us think it's a threat."

With guys like Donaldson and Letterman failing to see reality, the hard-core S-P shock troops become even bolder. Take, for example, Denver mayor John Hickenlooper, who actually removed the words "Merry Christmas" from a display at City Hall. After a huge outcry,

Hickenlooper backed down, but, believe me, he didn't want to. There are scores of other examples that make the Christmas-controversy deniers look foolish.

In addition to Letterman and Donaldson, Jon Stewart weighed in, addressing my concerns on **The Daily Show:** "Bill O'Reilly thinks there's a war on Christmas . . . If Bill O'Reilly needs to feel persecuted, here's my Kwanzaa gift to Bill O'Reilly: Make me your enemy. I, Jon Stewart, hate Christmas."

Stewart was joking (sort of), but the message was clear: O'Reilly's a buffoon. Don't believe him.

But the TV guys were absolutely gentle in the criticisms of me compared to the newspapers. They went **wild**!

The **New York Times** ran three separate opinion pieces calling me all kinds of names and pretty much assigning me to hell (again, figuratively; S-Ps don't really believe in hell, although they might make an exception in my case). **Times** columnist Nicholas Kristof went completely off the rails, implying I was another Mullah Omar: "Perhaps I'm particularly sensitive to religious hypocrites because I've spent a chunk of time abroad watching Muslim versions of Mr. O'Reilly—demagogic table-thumpers who exploit public religiosity as a cynical ploy to gain attention and money."

Kristof then went on to compare me to Father Coughlin, the far-right radical radio priest in the Depression, and communist blacklist-era scourge Senator Joseph McCarthy. I assume he was saving Hitler and Stalin for a follow-up column. By the way, in an interesting aside, a few months after his initial attacks on me, which included a rant that I didn't care enough about the Darfur atrocities in the Sudan, Kristoff was put in a delicate situation. The **New York Times** accepted close to a million dollars to run advertisements from Sudanese interests. Wow! What about Darfur, Nick, what say you about those ads? Mullah Omar would like to know.

Kristof, the S-P culture warrior, refused to comment. In fact, ol' Nick never did agree to debate me. Instead, he went on the Bill Maher program and leveled some cheap shots my way. That's a common S-P tactic: avoid face-to-face encounters, snipe from afar.

Anyway, back to the good tidings about Christmas. Kristof's coworker at the **Times,** Adam Cohen, no relation to the aforementioned Randy, took up a different theme: "The Christmas that Mr. O'Reilly and his allies are promoting—one closely aligned with retailers, with a smack-down attitude toward non-believers—fits with their campaign to make America more like a theocracy, with Christian displays on public property and Christian prayer in public schools."

Of course, that is absolute rubbish. Cohen just made it up. As I have made abundantly clear on my programs, I have no interest in forcing religion on retailers, Christian prayer in public schools, or any other kind of "theocratic" display. Like his namesake Randy, Adam Cohen is a rank propagandist, and he's not alone.

About a hundred miles down I-95, **Philadelphia Inquirer** columnist writer Jeff Gelles also distorted a few things: "I address [my comments] to Fox News' Bill O'Reilly: Please quit claiming there's a war on Christmas and threatening to boycott businesses just because some tell customers 'Happy Holidays' instead of 'Merry Christmas.' "

Of course, as you probably know, there was no boycott threat. Gelles picked that misinformation up from Joel Stein, writing erroneously in the **Los Angeles Times:** "In fact, [John] Gibson and fellow Fox anchor Bill O'Reilly are so upset that they have organized a boycott of Target, Wal-Mart, Kmart, Sears, and Costco for using the words 'Happy Holidays' in their ads. . . ."

Two days later, the **Los Angeles Times** issued this correction (which apparently Jeff Gelles missed): "A Dec. 6 column by Joel Stein said that Fox News' Bill O'Reilly and John Gibson had 'organized a boycott' of stores . . . they have not called for a boycott."

But the Christmas hits just kept on coming:

The **Philadelphia Inquirer,** apparently crazed by the Christmas controversy, editorialized this way: "Now O'Reilly gripes that the commercializers aren't exploiting Jesus' name aggressively enough to sell Obsession and Xbox 360."

Associated Press writer Frazier Moore, a committed S-P trooper, chimed in: "O'Reilly is the sort of guy for whom the expression 'stuff it' was invented, eh Santa?"

Hard-core left-wing editorial writer Cynthia Tucker had a very interesting take in the **Atlanta Journal-Constitution:** "The oddest thing about this cultural imbroglio is the insistence by some Christian purists that stores—palaces of consumerism—should observe the season with declarations of 'Merry Christmas.' "

That's right, Cynthia, it would be nice if the American stores that prohibit the words "Merry Christmas" would stop doing that. After all, most people are buying **Christmas** gifts, madam, so it's not at all "odd" to respect the public holiday that generates the gift-giving, especially in a place that is profiting from it.

For the record, there are many misguided

journalists in America, but Cynthia Tucker may top the list. Her giveaway expression "Christian purists" is about as condescending as it gets.

But the height of the print-press nuttiness was reached in the **Washington Post.** In a column rhapsodizing about Irving Berlin, Harold Meyerson rallied the S-P forces with this final paragraph: "Now the Fox News demagogues want to impose a more sectarian Christmas on us, supplanting the distinctly American holiday we have celebrated lo [lo?] these three score years with a holiday that divides us along religious lines. Bill O'Reilly can blaspheme all he wants but, like millions of my countrymen, I take attacks on Irving Berlin's America personally. If O'Reilly doesn't like it here, why doesn't he go back to where he came from?"

Lo, Harold, that would be Levittown.

Attacks on Irving Berlin's America? Easy on the eggnog, Bud—I am an Irving fan. He wrote the song "White Christmas" when he could have called it "White Holiday." (He also wrote "God Bless America," when he could have called it "We Like America.") Irving Berlin seems to be a Christmas kind of guy. Meyerson seems to be, well, a bit unhinged.

After a while, this semicoherent nonsense got boring as the list of newspaper people decrying my reporting on Christmas went on and on and on; the media lemmings were jumping off the secular cliff in astounding numbers.

But at the same time that these S-P newspaper zombies were imputing false motives to me feverishly at their computers, some curious things were happening in the real world. On the fifth day of Christmas, pollsters were polling and Congress was voting.

On that day, December 20, 2005, while scores of press people were denying any Christmas controversy even existed, a CNN/**USA Today**/ Gallup Poll was released. The CNN.com article went this way:

> 69% [of those polled] said they prefer "Merry Christmas" over "happy holidays," which garnered 29%.
>
> Compared with the 2004 Christmas [or do I mean holiday?] season, the number of people who said they use "happy holidays" had dropped 12%, from 41% to 29%.
>
> That's bound to be good news for some Christian conservatives who've been pushing for advertisers and stores to wish patrons "Merry Christmas" rather than the more secular and less specific "happy holidays."
>
> On the political front, although the campaign for "Merry Christmas" appears to be waged largely by conservative Americans,

many Democrats and liberals were also affected, according to the poll.

The majority of liberals and a majority of Democrats said they preferred "happy holidays" last year. But this year, a majority of liberals and a majority of Democrats said their preference was "Merry Christmas."

You best believe Santa Claus was happy with that poll, but the media was not. In addition, the poll affords us a perfect opportunity to analyze the secular bias CNN puts out there every day (and that **USA Today** is buying into).

First, CNN's assertion that "Christian conservatives" were behind the movement to respect Christmas is deceptive. While a few mainly Protestant groups did, indeed, make it a cause, the real pressure was put on by millions of independent Americans who simply like, respect, and enjoy the Christmas tradition.

I know CNN will be shocked, but Americans of all faiths and political persuasions are angry about the denigration of Christmas. As the poll numbers prove, this is a mass annoyance.

Then there is CNN's phrasing: "the more secular and inclusive 'happy holidays.' " They got the secular part right (they're experts in that field), but to say that "happy holidays" is more "inclusive" is fallacious in the extreme. Polls show that 95 percent of Americans celebrate Christmas and 84 percent describe themselves as Christians, according to a study by **U.S. News & World Report.** So anything that is specific to that enormous group, like the words "Merry Christmas," would certainly be "inclusive," would it not?

If CNN had a clue, it might be dangerous.

Even as the secular press was gnashing its collective teeth over the poll on the nonexistent controversy, the House of Representatives was ramping up and weighing in on the bogus issue. Again, for a "fabricated" situation, this Christmas deal was getting an awful lot of attention.

In December 2005, House Resolution 579 was introduced on the floor of the 109th Congress. It stated:

> Resolution: Expressing the sense of the House of Representatives that the symbols and traditions of Christmas should be protected.
>
> Whereas Christmas is a national holiday celebrated on December 25; and Whereas the Framers intended that the First Amendment to the Constitution of the United

States would prohibit the establishment of religion, not prohibit any mention of religion or reference to God in civic dialog: Now, therefore, be it Resolved, That the House of Representatives—

1) Recognizes the importance of the symbols and traditions of Christmas;
2) Strongly disapproves of attempts to ban references to Christmas; and
3) Expresses support for the use of these symbols and traditions.

The vote to approve the Resolution to Protect Christmas Symbols and Traditions was 401 to 22, with 5 voting simply "present." All the dissenters are Democrats: Gary Ackerman (NY), Earl Blumenauer (OR), Lois Capps (CA), Emanuel Cleaver (MO), Diana DeGette (CO), Jane Harman (CA), Alcee Hastings (FL), Michael Honda (CA), Barbara Lee (CA), John Lewis (GA), Jim McDermott (WA), George Miller (CA), Gwen Moore (WI), James Moran (VA), Donald Payne (NJ), Bobby Rush (IL), Janice Schakowsky (IL), Bobby Scott (VA), Fortney Stark (CA), Debbie Wasserman Schultz (FL), Robert Wexler (FL), and Lynn Woolsey (CA).

Most of those congresspeople cited "separation of church and state" as the reason for their nay vote. But now you know who the most secular members of the House really are.

In the end, Christmas won a big victory in Congress, in the department stores, in the polls, and in the court of public opinion. The jaded, secular press got its butt kicked, which, of course, is a good thing. Still, I'm going to give the last word on the Christmas controversy to the ultraliberal **Baltimore Sun**, which on December 2, 2005, ran this headline:

ACLU Says No War on Christmas!

Well, that certainly settles it once and for all. My special thanks to the **Baltimore Sun** for its fair and balanced coverage.

Ironically, four months after the House voted to uphold the traditions of Christmas, a secretary working for the St. Paul, Minnesota, city council was told to take down some decorations she had put up in her workspace: Easter eggs, the Easter bunny, and a sign that said "Happy Easter." The woman did as she was told. The powers that be in St. Paul told the media that any symbol of Easter might be offensive around the Easter season, even though no one complained.

I immediately asked a startled St. Paul city councilman on the air if St. Paul was also going to change its name. After all, the city takes its name from a saint. That would be Paul. Maybe a non-Christian would be offended by the city's name. I suggested that St. Paul, Minnesota, should be renamed "Paul's a Good Guy, Minnesota."

In the wake of that interview, a few hundred miles down the Mississippi River, **St. Louis Post-Dispatch** columnist John Sonderegger, a big S-P guy, chose to revisit the Christmas controversy during Easter. Don't ask me why. Anyway, Sonderegger wrote, "Yes, you can make [Christmas] into a very religious occasion. . . . That's fine for some. But for the rest of us in America, Christmas is our annual Feel-Good Holiday."

"Feel-Good Holiday"? "[F]or the rest of us in America"? Somebody inform Sonderegger and the **St. Louis Post-Dispatch** that eight out of ten "of us" are Christian and celebrate Christmas as a "religious occasion."

But in the interest of **inclusion** I suggest that we allow the S-P movement to celebrate their version of Christmas. Let's call it "Feel Good Day." And a Happy Feel Good Day to you!

To wrap up this chapter on the victorious battle for Christmas (sorry, Easter), let's turn to President Calvin Coolidge. Ol' Cal did not stand silent (historical reference) on the merits of Christmas. On December 25, 1927, he sent this message:

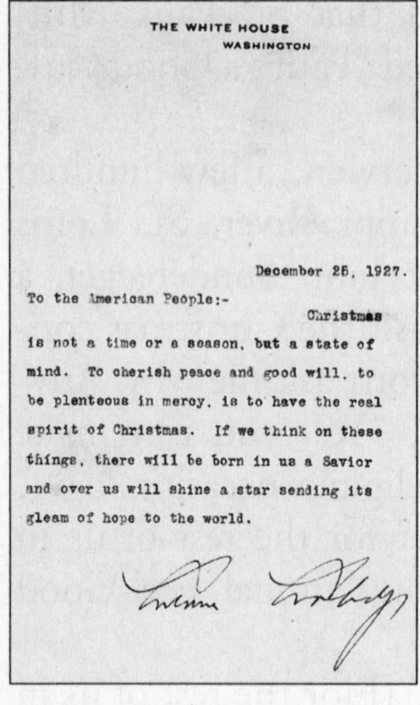

THE WHITE HOUSE
WASHINGTON

December 25, 1927.

To the American People:-

Christmas is not a time or a season, but a state of mind. To cherish peace and good will, to be plenteous in mercy, is to have the real spirit of Christmas. If we think on these things, there will be born in us a Savior and over us will shine a star sending its gleam of hope to the world.

Calvin Coolidge

A Christmas message from President Coolidge.

To the American People: Christmas is not a time or a season, but a state of mind. To cherish peace and good will, to be plenteous in mercy, is to have the real spirit of Christmas. If we think on these things, there will be born in us a Savior and over us will shine a star sending its gleam of hope to the world.

Calvin Coolidge, how could you?

Six

Ambushed: Other Battles Reconsidered

It ain't over 'til you're stupid.

—**THE ART OF CULTURE WAR,** O'REILLY TZU

Not all culture battles go as well as the Christmas controversy. Sometimes I lose. Not often, but sometimes, and it galls me.

Here's a sad example. In the late summer of 2003, I traveled to Los Angeles for the annual Book Expo, which is kind of a booksellers' convention where various authors give bookstore owners a heads-up on their upcoming works. My new book back then—**Who's Looking Out for You?**—was to be released in October, and I had agreed to speak on a panel with Molly Ivins and Al Franken, who also had books coming out. Some people thought I was nuts to do this, since both writers are far left. But I have no problem with Ms. Ivins. She's a dedicated progressive but not an unpleasant individual. As for Franken, I had tangled with him before and, although I did not respect him, I felt no need to avoid him. He was just another rabid show business liberal with a mean streak.

What I didn't know was that Franken had written a book that featured me on the cover with the word "liar" beneath my name. I found this out literally minutes before the panel discussion was to begin; a much larger-than-life reproduction of the cover was set up in the lobby as a promotional come-on. And the picture the publisher used of me was doctored to make me look hideous! In hindsight, I should have excused myself and left the dais, because this was a pure blindside play. Nobody had informed me about the nature of Franken's book, although the moderator, former congresswoman Patricia Schroeder, certainly knew about it, as did the panel's organizers.

But I did not leave the dais. I decided to confront the situation, although unarmed and unarmored because I had no idea what was in Franken's book. How dumb was that? The huge lurid cover did not suggest that Franken was looking out for me, and as everybody knows, the guy is an accomplished smear merchant. I was off-the-charts dumb to put myself in that position. Remember this: Stupidity in the culture war can get you hurt.

Anyway, I gave my presentation first, which just added to the setup, and simply said that my book did not attack anyone or call them names. **Who's Looking Out for You?**—which wound up selling more than a million copies—is an honest attempt to help everyday Americans prosper; there is no ideological theme to the book.

Then Al Franken rose to begin his diatribe, and I took his measure. He had failed on television with a sitcom called **Lateline.** He had bombed in the movies with a film based on his **Saturday Night Live** character "Stuart Smalley." But he had finally found a prosperous niche as a far-left pundit whose main weapon was character assassination. His modus operandi was calling people with whom he disagreed, like Rush Limbaugh, sophomoric names. And when critics called him out for such immature vitriol, Franken would fall back on the defense that his work was intended to be "satire." Jonathan Swift would be made physically ill by the assertion.

Franken had (and continues to have) access to the mainstream media, especially to the print press, CNN, NPR, and the late-night talk shows. He had made good money with his Limbaugh attack book, but then had bombed with a book touting himself for president. Now he was back on smear row.

As Franken began speaking, I simply couldn't believe it. The guy told the audience that I was a pathological liar and had even lied about where I grew up. His presentation was based on a passage in his book:

> See, O'Reilly always likes to crow about his hardscrabble childhood in working class Levittown, Long Island . . . Trouble is, an inside source [O'Reilly's mother] tells a different story. Mrs. O'Reilly proudly told the **Washington Post** that the family regularly took vacations in Florida, and that little Billy attended private school, private college, and that their home was in the affluent suburb of Westbury, not blue-collar Levittown.

On the opposite page is the mortgage deed to the house my parents bought more than fifty years ago, the house in which I was raised. You'll notice the deed says "Levittown."

But far worse than Franken's deliberate lie about my upbringing was his reference to my mother. She has, tragically, been suffering from dementia for years and for that reason has round-the-clock supervision. Al Franken never talked with my mother or to anyone else who knows my background. He simply put forth absolute falsehoods in his book without the decency to check the record. I can say this with absolute certainty: The man is truly a loath-

Form LL-40
COUNTY TRUST CO.
V. A. Bond — Blank

V. A. 269

Parcel No. 4848

Bank No. 28961

Know all Men by these Presents, that

WILLIAM J. O'REILLY and WINIFRED ANGELA O'REILLY, his wife

residing at Levittown, New York,

hereinafter designated as the obligors, do hereby acknowledge the obligors to be justly indebted to **THE COUNTY TRUST COMPANY,** a banking corporation organized under the laws of the State of New York, having its principal place of business at 235 Main Street, White Plains, New York, hereinafter referred to and designated herein as the Mortgagee, in the sum of SEVEN THOUSAND FIVE HUNDRED NINETY AND 00/100 Dollars ($ 7,590.00) lawful money of the United States, which sum said obligors do hereby covenant to pay to said mortgagee, its successors or assigns, with interest thereon at the rate of four per centum (4%) per annum as follows:

BY PAYMENT on the first day of March, 1951 of the sum of $ 15.28 and thereafter in payments of THIRTY SIX AND 28/100 - - - - - - - - - - - - - - Dollars ($ 36.28) on the first day of each subsequent month until the principal and interest are fully paid, except that the final payment of the entire indebtedness evidenced hereby, if not sooner paid, shall be due and payable on the first day of February, 1961. Each of said payments when received by the holder hereof, shall be applied first to the payment of interest computed from the date hereof, and thereafter from the last date to which interest shall have been paid at the rate of four per centum (4%) per annum, on the unpaid balance of the principal sum thereof and the remainder in the reduction of principal.

The parties hereto intend that payment of $ 4,554.00 of said indebtedness shall be guaranteed under the Servicemen's Readjustment Act of 1944 as amended. Such Act and Regulations issued thereunder, and in effect on the date hereof, shall govern the rights, duties, and liabilities of the parties hereto. Any provisions of this or other instruments executed in connection with said indebtedness which are inconsistent with said Act or Regulations are hereby amended to conform thereto. In the event that said indebtedness shall be declared to be ineligible for such guarantee at any time (written statement of the Administrator or any authorized agent of the Administrator or the Veteran's Administration to that effect to be deemed conclusive proof of such ineligibility) the then holder of this instrument may, at its option, declare all sums secured hereby immediately due and payable. Said indebtedness may be prepaid in the manner provided by said Regulations.

All sums due under this bond and the mortgage securing this bond are payable at the office of the mortgagee at 64 North Broadway, Tarrytown, New York, in lawful money as aforesaid.

AND IT IS HEREBY EXPRESSLY AGREED that the whole of said principal shall become due at the option of the said mortgagee, or the successors or assigns of the mortgagee, after default in the payment of any installment of principal when due, or of interest for fifteen days, or of any payment comprising both interest and amortization for fifteen days, or after default in the making of any deposit on account of taxes, insurance and/or water charges for fifteen days, if such deposits are herein provided for, or after default in the payment of any tax, water rate, assessments, or other lien or charge for thirty days after same shall become due and payable, or after any other default, or upon the happening of any event by which, in any case, under the terms of the mortgage securing this bond, the said principal sum may or shall become due and payable; also that all the covenants and agreements made by the said obligors in the mortgage covering premises therein described and collateral hereto are hereby made part of this instrument.

Signed and sealed this 26th day of February, 1951 .

In the presence of: Charles D. Eginton

William J. O'Reilly ..........L.S.
William J. O'Reilly

Winifred Angela O'Reilly ..........L.S.
Winifred Angela O'Reilly

....L.S.

Here is the deed to the modest house in which I grew up in Levittown—repeat: Levittown.

some individual. Anyone who believes anything out of his mouth is a fool.

For the record, both my late father and I worked brutally hard so I could attend a Catholic high school and Marist College, which was not an expensive school back then. My dad worked a tedious, dead-end office job; I painted houses. My family did go to Florida once . . . on a Greyhound bus. My face peeled on the long ride home.

Unfortunately, back at the "literary" panel, I had to sit there and listen to Franken lying about my life. Of course, my Irish temper flared (that's its job) and, when he was finished, I attempted to issue a rebuttal, but he interrupted me. With that provocation, I told him, in no uncertain terms, to shut up. Truthfully, I wanted to beat the you-know-what out of him. Now, whenever you get to that point in a confronta-

And here I am as a kid with my father alongside that house.

tion, you are probably going to lose. The proof follows. . . .

C-SPAN taped this whole sorry spectacle and Franken ran with it, parlaying the confrontation into massive publicity that made his vile book into a bestseller. The media, naturally, greeted Franken's assertions with glee, and I was put completely on the defensive. When Fox News filed against him in court for trademark infringement, Franken got even more publicity and media backslaps.

To borrow **National Review** columnist Mona Charen's description, Al Franken is a "useful idiot." The secular-progressive leadership loves him. He, along with **New York Times** columnist Frank Rich, is their chief character assassin. Franken is a man without scruples, a far-left fanatic whose brand of unbridled hatred is sound-bite ready and media friendly. If the S-Ps were ever to succeed in America, Al Franken and people like him would actually be even more prominent. How frightening is that?

I firmly believe that karma will take care of Franken. His 2004 follow-up book fell far below expectations (his publisher Dutton got what it deserved), and his radio operation, Air America, is a commercial disaster. There is justice in the universe and it will visit this guy. Wait and see.

I didn't even want to sully this book with Franken's name, but he did teach me something: In the culture war, there is no Geneva Convention. No rules are honored on the secular-progressive side (and, to be fair, there are traditionalists who do sink into the mud as well). The S-Ps are capable of doing just about anything. And if traditionalists don't understand that, they will eventually lose the fight. Al Franken won a round against this culture warrior by using blatant dishonesty and a crafty media strategy. It won't happen again.

As part of the war plan, it should be understood and emphasized that any mistake, misstatement, or miscalculation will hurt the traditional culture warrior, and these are largely self-inflicted wounds. In my case, I do three hours of commentary every weekday (one on TV, two on the radio), and mistakes are going to happen. And when they do, the S-P smear Web sites, which obsessively tape every word I say, gleefully spit out the errors to the public. Again, I'm not whining, just reporting. This is the terrain of the culture war. The truth is, I shouldn't make factual errors or misspeak ever. But it happens—and when it does, we try to correct the record quickly.

There are other types of errors, however, and these are harder to excuse. I've lost a few culture battles because of my **demeanor,** and that is simply not acceptable in a war as intense as this one.

The best example of my demeanor foolishness was an episode with Terry Gross, who hosts a radio program on NPR called **Fresh Air.** Ms. Gross is a smart, liberal woman who seems overly sympathetic to the secular-progressive cause. Nevertheless, I accepted an invitation to appear on her program to promote **Who's Looking Out for You?** This was another dopey move by me in an autumn full of them.

Ms. Gross called me at my radio studio, and we spoke briefly and cordially before the interview began. But once the tape was rolling, she shifted gears with a vengeance. Instead of asking about my book and ideas, Ms. Gross used the interview to promote Al Franken's gibberish by questioning me about his accusations (and others made in **Harper's** magazine). For about fifty minutes I answered Gross's queries about my "lying," but finally, when she began quoting other people who were bad-mouthing me from within the S-P ranks, I terminated the interview by saying this on the air:

"We've spent fifty minutes, all right, of me defending defamation against me in every possible way, while you gave Al Franken a complete pass on his defamatory book. And if you think that's fair, Terry, then you need to get in another business. I'll tell you right now and I'll tell your listeners, if you have the courage to put this on the air, this is basically an unfair interview, designed to try to trap me into saying something **Harper's** [magazine] can use. And you know it. You should be ashamed of yourself. And that is the end of this interview."

Because we had taped the chat at the studio I use for **The Radio Factor**, I could play the entire interview on the radio and TV without Ms. Gross or her producers editing it. I also posted it on my Web site, BillOreilly.com. More than 1 million people listened to the conversations on the Web site alone.

Terry Gross sandbagged me on her NPR show **Fresh Air.**

A few days later Jeffrey Dvorkin, the ombudsman in charge of addressing controversies at the National Public Radio network, issued this stinging rebuke to Terry Gross:

"I believe the listeners were not well served by this interview. It may have illustrated the 'cultural wars' that seem to be flaring in this country. Unfortunately, the interview only served to confirm the belief, held by some, in NPR's liberal bias. It left the impression that there was something not quite right about the reasons behind this program . . ."

So another win for the good guys, right? S-P sympathizer Terry Gross was dressed down by her own ombudsman, who exposed her for the left-wing ideologue she is. But if you read on, you will see, unfortunately, how the great culture warrior O'Reilly snatched defeat from the jaws of victory.

About a year after my first confrontation with Ms. Gross, she brought her own book to market. Titled **All I Did Was Ask,** it chronicled her interviews with famous people . . . like me. I invited Ms. Gross on **The Factor,** knowing in advance that she would be in a bad place if she did agree to appear because **she did not even mention the ombudsman's scolding in her book!**

Truthfully, I was surprised when Terry Gross agreed to come on **The Factor.** How could she defend such a blatant omission? All I had to do was ask my questions without rancor. I do that, she's toast. Terry Gross would be exposed on national TV as either a woman trying to hide something or a first-rate weaselette.

The segment began and, after a brief setup, I immediately cut to the chase:

O'Reilly: "Why wouldn't you put in your book that you were scolded by your own ombudsman? You left that out? Why did you leave it out?"

Gross: "I don't know why I left it out."

O'Reilly: "You don't **know**?"

Gross: "The point, Bill, is that I think the interview was very fair . . ."

O'Reilly: "Those were 'do you beat your wife' questions, Terry."

Gross: "No, they weren't."

O'Reilly: "Well, the ombudsman says they were."

Gross: "I disagree. That's not exactly what he said."

O'Reilly: "You want me to quote it? It's pretty bad."

Gross: "Go ahead."

O'Reilly: "All right. [I read the ombudsman's quote.] 'Halfway through the interview, it felt as though Terry Gross was indeed carrying Al Franken's water.' That's pretty embarrassing, Terry."

Gross: "I'm not embarrassed, because I disagree with him."

Now, **reading** that interview, most people would agree that Terry Gross was smoked. The problem was that on TV, I was mean to her. I snarled at the woman. I let her have it.

I lost.

In fact, thanks to me, even some who dislike Ms. Gross felt sorry for her. She's about five feet tall, wears glasses, and looks like a librarian. And there's this six-foot-four-inch, 200-pound O'Reilly guy banging her over the head. Dumb. A guy like Franken you can impale. Nobody's gonna feel sorry for an individual of that low caliber. But you can't browbeat a tiny female radio announcer. Even though the woman had no case, my strident tone transformed her into a sympathetic figure. Many casual viewers would remember one thing above all in that segment: O'Reilly was mean to a woman. Mean, mean, mean.

So you see that fighting this culture war is complicated, fraught with danger, and exhausting. The warrior in defense of tradition needs to be sharp, well informed, and aware of not only the facts but also of tone and demeanor during the debate. Anything the culture warrior says can—and **will**—be used against him or her.

But we have no choice as far as culture war is concerned. It desperately needs to be fought, because today the stakes are as high as they get. Especially when dealing with a far more brutal conflict: the war on terror.

Seven

The Culture War and the War on Terror

George W. Bush is the greatest terrorist in the world.

—HARRY BELAFONTE

Who do you think Osama bin Laden supports in the American culture war: the traditionalists or the secular-progressives?

Not so fast. . . . This may be a trick question.

On the one hand, the Saudi-born terrorist despises just about everything the S-Ps fervently espouse: a de-emphasis of religion, a libertine social landscape, no judgments on most private behavior, and an acceptance of human weakness.

For those of you not currently up to date on their policies, al-Qaeda would decapitate gays who wanted to marry, cut off the hands of drug abusers, stone to death anyone who suggested Allah not be included in the public arena, and blind anyone who looked at pornography. If Osama was calling the shots in the United

States, the ACLU would be, in theory, very, very busy. In reality, they'd be dead.

But think about what I am about to put forth: From his hideout somewhere in the Muslim world, Osama bin Laden and his cohorts have got to be cheering on the S-P movement, because its most fanatical adherents are opposed to the bedrock strengths of traditional America. The S-P worldview is much softer than that of the traditional forces, as I'll demonstrate shortly. For now, it is important to understand that the S-P vanguard, the ACLU, has actively opposed just about every anti-terror strategy the U.S. government has introduced. In my view, that opposition greatly helps al-Qaeda and other terrorist outfits.

The secular-progressive movement opposes coerced interrogation—not torture, but harsh treatment—of captured terror suspects. They object to detention of them at U.S. military prisons like Guantánamo Bay. In addition, the ACLU opposes military tribunals (rather than civilian trials) to determine the guilt or innocence of suspected terrorists, rendition programs where terror suspects are held in foreign countries, floating wiretaps (already in use in U.S. criminal investigations), telephone surveillance of overseas calls by U.S. spy agencies, airport profiling, the Patriot Act, the war in Iraq, and random bag searches on subway or mass-transit systems.

In short, the ACLU opposes making life more difficult for terrorists but proposes absolutely nothing to make Americans safer. Osama has got to love it.

On the positive side (sarcasm intended), the ACLU supports: Constitutional protections for noncitizen terror suspects captured overseas, Geneva Convention protections for terror suspects captured wearing civilian clothing (which, of course, eliminates them from the Geneva Convention treaties), civilian lawyers and criminal due process instead of military justice, and the exposure of top-secret U.S. antiterror programs in the press.

There's more. According to the ACLU, government officials should be prosecuted for the alleged exposure of former CIA agent Valerie Plame, but at the same time no government official should be investigated for leaking information about the top-secret National Security Agency's overseas listening activities, approved by President Bush under the seal of an Executive Order.

Add it all up and you can see exactly what I meant earlier: When it comes to the war on terror, Osama bin Laden has got to be thrilled that he has unwitting allies in the ACLU and, indeed, the entire S-P movement. In my assessment, the S-Ps fail to see the danger clearly. They constantly harp on America's mistakes while confronting violent terrorism, but they do not put forth viable solutions to neutralize the threats. They create a fog that damages our counterterrorism efforts. If all Americans bought into the ACLU's terror platform, instead of hiding in a Pakistani cave someplace, Osama might be sitting at a negotiating table in Paris, patiently awaiting an interview with **Le Monde.**

I know I'll be harshly criticized for writing that last paragraph, but as I asked, think about it. How could any sane person adopt the stance the ACLU takes toward the war on terror? Don't those people get 9/11? Doesn't the S-P movement understand the danger America faces from terrorist fanatics who would use nuclear weapons, should they acquire them, against us?

The answer to that question is a bit complicated, but it is rooted in the one thing that the secular-progressive movement and Al Qaeda have in common: Both outfits believe that the United States of America is fundamentally a bad place.

Again, I'll be criticized for writing that, so let's back it up and return to our pal George Lakoff, the premier S-P philosopher and guru. Like most S-P true believers, Lakoff believes that the

United States is at least partially responsible for the buildup of worldwide terrorism; therefore, by that reasoning, it was some of America's own doing that it was attacked on 9/11. That point of view is obviously a tough sell to the American public, so the ACLU and others do not bring the hypothesis up very often.

But Lakoff makes the S-P position crystal clear on page 66 of his **Elephant** book:

> The idealistic claim of the Bush administration is that they intend to wipe out all terrorism. What is not mentioned is that the United States has systematically promoted a terrorism of its own and has trained terrorists, from the contras to the mujahideen, the Honduran death squads, and the Indonesian military. Will the U.S. government stop training terrorists? Of course not. It will deny that it does so . . . if the United States wants terror to end, the United States must end its own contribution to terror.

So the war on terror is largely America's fault, according to Lakoff, who conveniently avoids mentioning America's fight against the expansion of worldwide communism. As any intelligent person knows, the brutal cold war against the Soviet Union and Red China was the primary reason the United States armed opponents of communism like the contras in Nicaragua and the mujahideen in Afghanistan.

This is so typical of Lakoff and other S-P "thinkers": They ignore all perspective in their analysis. When was the last time you heard any S-P fanatic mention that almost 3 million people were slaughtered by communist forces in Southeast Asia after the United States withdrew from Vietnam? I've never heard Jane Fonda, a duchess of the S-P realm, mention that, have you?

The bedrock belief that America is, and has been, an evil country is crucial to understanding the secular-progressive point of view when it comes to the war on terror. Here's their bankrupt reasoning: The S-Ps cannot support any antiterror measures until the United States stops being a terrorist country itself. Get it? Yes, they're serious. If you don't believe me, travel to Berkeley, California, or Cambridge, Massachusetts, and ask.

I first came across this thinking when I interviewed a man named Jeremy Glick on **The Factor** shortly after the attack on 9/11. Mr. Glick's father had been murdered in the collapse of the World Trade Center. Despite that tragedy, however, Jeremy had signed his name to an advertisement paid for by a radical S-P group called

Not in Our Name. Part of that ad suggested an outrageous equivalency: "We too watched with shock the horrific events of September 11th. We too mourned the thousands of innocent dead in Baghdad, Panama City, and a generation ago, Vietnam."

Wow. Comparing the 9/11 attack, which resulted in the murders of about three thousand innocent civilians, to the defeat of Saddam Hussein in the first Gulf War (remember, he invaded Kuwait and brutalized the people there), to the removal of Panamanian dictator Manuel Noriega (who had turned his country into an international narcotics shipping center), and to the U.S. involvement in Vietnam (a war that was fought to prevent the spread of totalitarianism and communism). I just couldn't believe a young man like Jeremy Glick was nutty enough to sign his name to that kind of a display. There must have been some sort of misunderstanding; maybe it was part of his grieving process.

Wrong, again, culture warrior.

In what has become a famous TV verbal shoot-out, Glick came on **The Factor** and told me my criticism of the ad was dead wrong. Moreover, he opined, my surprise at his participation was naïve:

"I'm actually surprised that you're surprised," Glick told me. "If you think about it, our current president, who I feel and many feel is in this position illegitimately by neglecting the voices of African Americans in the Florida coup . . . our current president now inherited a legacy from his father and inherited a political legacy that's responsible for training militarily, economically, and situating geopolitically the parties involved in the alleged assassination and murder of my father and countless of others."

The **alleged** assassination of his father? Glick was asserting that not only was the Bush administration partially responsible for the murderous actions of al-Qaeda, they also might even have had something **directly** to do with them, by supporting groups like the mujahideen in the past.

Now, when you get a misguided individual like Jeremy Glick on television, you simply cannot allow him to spout unproved accusations and downright slander. If you do that, your audience will turn on you. Add in the suffering Glick's words could bring to others who lost loved ones on 9/11, and you have to pull the plug. Which I did. Glick got the boot after this exchange:

Glick: "You evoke 9/11 to rationalize everything from domestic plunder to imperialistic aggression worldwide. You evoke sympathy with the 9/11 families."

O'Reilly: "That's a bunch of crap. I've done more for the 9/11 families, by their own admission, than you will ever hope to do."

Glick: "Okay."

O'Reilly: "So keep your mouth shut when you sit here exploiting those people."

Glick: "Well, you're not representing me."

O'Reilly: "I'd never represent you."

Glick: "Why?"

O'Reilly: "Because you have a warped view of this world and a warped view of this country."

Glick: "Well, explain that."

O'Reilly: "All right. You didn't support the action against Afghanistan to remove the Taliban. You were against it, okay?"

Glick: "Why would I want to brutalize and further punish the people in Afghanistan?"

Why, indeed, when the whole thing was America's fault from the get-go? That's Glick-think taken directly from the George Lakoff playbook. It was pathetic.

Subsequently, thanks to me, Jeremy Glick became an icon of the S-P movement, which celebrated his "bravery" in standing up to the barbarian O'Reilly.

A few years later, the S-Ps tried the same trick with Cindy Sheehan, whose son Casey, a dedicated professional American soldier, was killed in the Iraq war. Ms. Sheehan, you may remember, demanded a meeting with President Bush even though she had already had one. But Ms. Sheehan wanted another chat after being tutored by antiwar zealots. Of course, Mr. Bush saw the trap a mile away. He rightly assumed Cindy Sheehan wanted to embarrass him and ignored the woman. Thereupon some in the media castigated the President for his "insensitivity" and made Cindy into a heroine.

The pro-Sheehan media blitz worked for a few weeks until I, convinced that the whole deal was a calculated S-P attack, played an audio clip of Ms. Sheehan telling Mark Knoller of CBS Radio that the terrorists in Iraq were "freedom fighters." She also said Israel was a terrorist nation. After that exposition, Ms. Sheehan's star dimmed as many rational folks who had sympathized with her, because of Casey, turned away.

The important point here is that the secular-progressive movement really believes Jeremy Glick and Cindy Sheehan are heroes. Worse, the S-Ps absolutely think the world's foremost problem is the evil superpower America, not Islamic fascist terror cells. If you take one thing away from this book, ladies and gentlemen, let it be that. The S-P brigades are not capable of understanding true evil. Their world perspective is so warped, it might even be downright dangerous.

A question then logically follows: How would the secular-progressives, themselves, deal with Islamic terrorism? Paging George Lakoff! He deals with that very issue on page 60 of his training manual:

> Most Islamic would be martyrs not only share [fanatical religious] beliefs but have also grown up in a culture of despair; they have nothing to lose. Eliminate such poverty and you eliminate the breeding ground for

> terrorists . . . when the Bush administration speaks of eliminating terror, it does not appear to be talking about eliminating cultures of despair and the social conditions that lead one to want to give up his life to martyrdom.

Outstanding. Lakoff apparently believes the United States has the power to eliminate poverty and change social conditions in places like Pakistan—estimated population, 163 million. America can't even eliminate poverty and change "social conditions" in Detroit, much less Islamabad. No government can impose prosperity or benign thinking on masses of people. It is simply impossible.

But George Lakoff and the S-Ps don't care for rational analysis. It sounds so good to say that terrorism can be defeated by a change in America's foreign policy. More Lakoff (page 63):

> What is needed is a new kind of moral foreign policy, one that realizes that America can only be a better America if the world is a better world. America must become a moral leader using fundamental human values: caring and responsibility carried out with strength to respond to the world's problems.

Once again, Lakoff seems to have missed the truth of America's great sacrifice in defeating the Soviet Union's totalitarianism and thereby bringing freedom to tens of millions of people in Eastern Europe and other Soviet-dominated areas. Nor does the S-P guru mention the enormous blood and treasure America spent defeating the Nazis and Imperial Japan. Don't those historic achievements fall in the category of "caring and responsibility carried out with strength to respond to the world's problems"? Or did the United States bring World War II upon itself as well?

It galls me that the S-Ps can get away with denigrating the United States when it, along with Great Britain and a precious few other countries, is standing up against a homicidal jihad that could destroy the world.

The S-Ps' unrealistic assessment of the war on terror is dangerous, naïve, and disqualifies the secular-progressive movement from any serious participation in the post-9/11 decision-making process. Sure, it would be great to heal social ills all over the world by waving a magic wand, but why bother spouting such delusional nonsense? The S-Ps are at their best when proposing airy theories or undermining policies with which they disagree. They fail dismally, however, when asked to create better, more effective policies to protect and improve the lives of everyday people. But that failure does not deter them; they are convinced they hold the moral high ground and those who oppose them—their enemies in the culture war—must be marginalized for the good of all.

And so I have arrived at this necessary conclusion: All clear-thinking Americans **should** become opponents of the S-P movement for the simple reason of self-preservation. If the secular-progressives ever come to power in America, and remember, Howard Dean got close, their policies would put you and your family in grave danger. Osama and his pals would love to face off against Lakoff, Dean, Michael Moore, George Soros, and the rest of the soft secular forces. In the 1930s, Adolf Hitler had a blast with Neville Chamberlain, the appeasement-supporting prime minister of Great Britain. That historical lesson might be worth revisiting in the culture war between the traditionalists and the S-Ps.

Oh, and one more thing. If you really want to see just how "caring" and humane the secular-progressive movement is, visit some of their black-hearted Web sites. If the hatred and libel you see are examples of S-P caring, somewhere the Marquis de Sade is cheering. One of the reasons I am writing this book is to show the great divide between how the S-Ps frame their arguments and their actual conduct. Many of these people are as ruthless as anyone you see in the Bush administration. But they hide behind the nurturing and enlightenment themes. To use an old Levittown expression: "What a crock."

Eight

Where's Mine?

God helps them that help themselves.

—**POOR RICHARD'S ALMANAC,** 1736

Way back in 1776, a committee that included Benjamin Franklin, John Adams, Thomas Jefferson, and others decided to include the Latin words **E Pluribus Unum** on the first Great Seal of the United States. Actually, a man named Pierre Eugene Du Simitiere came up with the idea. I have no idea who that man was, but great name, right?

The motto **E Pluribus Unum** means "From Many, One," thereby reflecting the integration of the thirteen colonies into one country. Subsequently, the words took on a deeper meaning as immigrants from all over the world brought their talents and energy and desire for freedom to the United States, fueling its rapid rise in power and prosperity. Yes, it's an old story that may have put you to sleep in high school. But it's worth thinking about. The United States is the strongest nation the world has ever seen because so "Many" pulled together to create the "One."

But in today's culture war, "From Many, One" no longer applies on the secular-progressive side. Their motto might be: "Where's Mine?" (**Ubi Est Meum?**) Remember, the S-Ps believe that the government has an obligation to **provide** Americans with prosperity and happiness. This philosophy is, of course, in direct conflict with the vision of the Founding Fathers. They did not want government to provide, they wanted it to get out of our way. They imagined and designed a system whereby freedom and capitalism would give most Americans an **opportunity** to pursue happiness. What you did with that **opportunity** was up to you.

Of course, it is certainly true that Americans born into poverty do not have the same opportunity as those born into wealth. There are also many other kinds of inequities (like innate intelligence) in play in America and everywhere else. In addition, as acknowledged earlier, the sad truth is that for more than two hundred years most black Americans were systematically deprived of the right to pursue happiness, and Native Americans were brutalized as America was being settled. Thus, the government today does owe African and Native Americans, and the poor in general, more attention and specific entitlement programs to help level the playing field. On that most traditionalists and S-Ps can agree.

But the S-P notion that the U.S. government has the right to seize private property (which is exactly what the estate tax achieves, for example, but under stealth wording), or redistribute legally earned income from the affluent to the poor, runs counter to the founding spirit of America in every way.

Look at the evidence. The United States became the strongest nation on earth because individuals working their butts off created a unified powerhouse. These individuals, from many different nations and backgrounds, bought into the idea of pursuing the American dream: That is, they chose to live an honest life that affords the individual and his/her family security and comfort backed by the freedom necessary for accomplishing these worthy goals. Americans fought and died for these principles. They are still fighting and dying today, liberating people from tyranny in Afghanistan and Iraq. Any erosion of the American ideal, which the secular-progressives are attempting by championing the entitlement state, would drastically weaken the nation.

Call me a crazy traditionalist, but I do not believe General George Soros could have defeated the Soviet Union or the Nazis or Tojo's fanatical

Japanese military. I don't believe that Howard Dean could command respect in any armed conflict and, most likely, would appease all over the place to avoid one in the first place.

Why do I believe so strongly that the secular-progressive movement is clueless as to how to deal with evil in the world? Simple. To them, as their leaders admit, evil doesn't really exist. Evil is actually redirected personal pain. Evil is a cry for help and can be persuaded to be good through kindness and caring. Stalin, Mao, and Hitler would all have changed direction if only Barbra Streisand could have sung "People Who Need People" to them in her very meaningful way.

Too harsh? No way.

History has demonstrated time and time again that disciplined, just societies prevail, while weak, utopian systems crash and burn. Life is tough, and we all have to deal with that, not buy into fantasies that could get us killed. The world is, and always has been, a struggle between good and evil. The Bible and the stark reality of the world teach us that. But as we all know, the Bible is not on the secular-progressive recommended reading list.

On the home front in America, traditional forces strongly believe that their hard-earned money is not the property of the government, to be distributed as largesse to others who, perhaps, are not willing to work to earn prosperity. On a personal note, I don't want my money being given to substance abusers, for example. Why should my money allow them to continue leading lives of dissolution? I donate money to drug and alcohol rehabilitation clinics like The Doe Fund, but I strenuously object to welfare payments for substance abusers to buy more substance. I work hard for my money and I don't want to support anyone who lives irresponsibly. Period.

Traditionalists like me understand that taxes are needed to keep the country strong and safe and to maintain an infrastructure that benefits the many. But cradle-to-grave entitlements, embraced fervently by the S-P movement, are rejected by traditionalists who understand that they foster weakness and sap initiative.

You only have to travel to Europe to see the difference that an entitlement culture makes. While the United States is a vibrant, creative, and exciting place, Europe today is largely stagnant. Workers there have little incentive to move ahead, because the rate of taxation is punishing and the governments guarantee a certain standard of living. In France, young people demonstrated for weeks because the government wanted a new law that would allow employers to actually fire them during the first two years of employment if they screwed up on a regular basis. But nooooo, we can't have that! The French sense of entitlement basically says "You owe me prosperity, government. You owe me." Where have we heard that before? Paging George Lakoff!

For those reasons and more, Europe has grown weak and frightened in the face of intense conflict, leaving it to America to protect them. And we do, even as the United States continues to grow economically and provide incredible opportunities for upward mobility (you are reading the words of the poster boy for U-M, by the way).

It is actually laughable to hear the S-Ps moan about economic injustice in the United States when we all know there is a flood of immigrants, both legal and illegal, trying to get into America. Surely, if the American system was as bad as the S-Ps claim, people would not be coming such great distances and at great risk to get into this country. So you can either believe your eyes or believe the S-P socialist propaganda. Up to you.

Sorry. Once again, I am applying real-world logic and facts to counter S-P propaganda. I've got to stop doing that. Don't tell Howard Dean. He'll call me another name. You see, loopy theory and delusional analysis are the twin pillars of the secular-progressive movement. Their theory, as we've seen over and over, essentially argues that every individual in this world is **owed** a certain lifestyle by the powers that be.

So once again, out with **E Pluribus, Unum.** That phrase is simply not nurturing enough. The brand-new S-P motto is inclusive, caring, and pithy: **Ubi Est Meum?** "Where's Mine?" If the S-Ps ever do take control of America, that phrase will ring loudly from sea to shining sea. Where Is Mine! I want it right **now**! And if I can't get stuff for myself, I'll take yours. I am owed prosperity even if I don't want to earn it.

Is that the kind of country in which you want to live? If so, France might be your next stop. By the way, the S-Ps love France. Says a lot about them. But then again, France is far away and many of us don't really care about it. What we do care about is our neighborhoods. So let's go there now.

PART 2

The Culture War Where You Live

Nine

The Battle for the Kids

Control the children and you control the future.

—THE ART OF CULTURE WAR, O'REILLY TZU

It was just another day in the San Juan Islands village of Friday Harbor, Washington (population: 2,000) when Sheriff Bill Cumming got a call that an elderly woman had been mugged. Apparently, two young men had knocked the lady to the ground, grabbed her purse, and run off. Since Friday Harbor is not exactly South Central Los Angeles, the sheriff had a good idea that a local troublemaker named Oliver Christensen may have been involved. There were only a few hellions in the little town and Christensen immediately became a suspect.

Sheriff Cumming also knew that Christensen, seventeen, was dating fourteen-year-old Lacey Dixon, a troubled young girl who lived at home with her single mother, Carmen Dixon. Doing what any good law-enforcement official would do, the sheriff called Mrs. Dixon and asked her to find out if her daughter had any knowledge of the crime.

The next time Oliver Christensen called the Dixon house, Lacey took her cordless phone into her bedroom and shut the door. But, unbeknownst to the girl, her mother snapped on the speakerphone in the kitchen and was taking notes. Sure enough, Christensen bragged to the fourteen-year-old that he had hidden the elderly woman's purse in some bushes.

Based partially upon the information Carmen Dixon subsequently provided authorities and her testimony in court, Christensen was convicted by a jury of second-degree robbery and sentenced to a couple of years in state prison. Subsequently, his conviction was upheld by a Washington State Appeals Court, but then the big guns of the secular army were brought in.

The ACLU, ignoring the actual crime, mounted an intense campaign to free Oliver Christensen based on the theory that Carmen Dixon had "violated" her daughter's privacy by listening to her phone conversation. ACLU lead attorney Douglas Kunder was blunt: "I don't think the state should be in the position of encouraging parents to act surreptitiously and eavesdrop on their children."

Disturbingly, the very liberal and secular Washington Supreme Court eventually sided with the ACLU and Christensen's conviction was overturned. The court ruled that the fourteen-year-old's privacy had, indeed, been violated and her mother had no legal right to the information she had gleaned from her daughter's conversation with the assailant. Carmen Dixon was stunned and told the media: "It's ridiculous! Kids have more rights than parents these days. My daughter was out of control, and that was the only way I could get information and keep track of her."

The prosecutor, Randall Gaylord, was also outraged: "I'm concerned that a fourteen-year-old's right to privacy now trumps the parent's right to be a parent."

Even the Associated Press, no bastion of traditional thought, began its news story on the court's decision this way: "In a victory for rebellious teenagers, the state Supreme Court ruled that a mother violated Washington's privacy law by eavesdropping on her daughter's phone conversation."

The state of Washington did retry Christensen, this time without Carmen Dixon's testimony. A jury again found him guilty, but he walked free after nine months in prison because the judge, Vickie Churchill, declined to give him more jail time. All of this skirmishing cost the taxpayers tens of thousands of dollars, and what did it really accomplish? Well, if you're in the S-P corps, it accomplished a lot for your side.

Remember, the ACLU is not an organization that does anything in a vacuum. The S-P spearhead knew exactly what it wanted to achieve when it marched into Carmen Dixon's life: that is, a court ruling demonstrating that a parent has no right to supervise a child surreptitiously. For the secular-progressive movement to achieve its goals in America, it must undermine traditional parental authority and convince children there's a brave new world out there that does not include being raised in the traditional way. The S-P goal is to diminish parental authority that, in the past, had been unquestioned.

This is a strategy—mentally separate children from their parents—that has been practiced by totalitarian governments all throughout history. In Nazi Germany, there was the Hitler Youth. Chairman Mao created the Children's Corps in Red China. Stalin and Castro rewarded children who spied on their parents. That's the blueprint. If you want to change a country's culture and traditions, children must first abandon them and embrace a new vision. Hello, secular-progressivism in the USA. I'm not saying these people are little Adolfs; I am saying they have adopted some totalitarian tactics in their strategies.

Another factor in the S-P vision for our kids is the development of sexual awareness at an early age. This strategy encourages children to mimic adult behavior and forge relationships outside the home. Thus, children separate themselves from parental influence earlier in life and are less likely to embrace the old-school values of their parents.

Here's a pretty amazing example of what I'm talking about. A few years ago in Los Angeles County, the Palmdale School District came up with an "educational" survey for students ages seven to ten. As part of that survey, the kids were asked to rate the following activities according to how often they experienced the thought or emotion:

- Touching my private parts too much.
- Thinking about having sex.
- Thinking about touching other people's private parts.
- Thinking about sex when I don't want to.
- Washing myself because I feel dirty inside.

Remember, these questions were put to kids as young as seven years old! Do you think about having sex? What the heck is going on?

Outraged, a group of Palmdale parents asked that exact question. But because school officials dodged and weaved, they couldn't get any answers. So the parents sued the district in federal court. The issue went all the way up to the Ninth Circuit Court of Appeals, the most liberal federal court in U.S. history. Predictably, the court ruled against the parents.

Judge Stephen Reinhardt, whose wife, Ramona Ripston, is the executive director of the ACLU in Southern California (can you believe this?), wrote the unanimous opinion, which stated that parents of public school children have no fundamental right to be the exclusive provider of sexual information to their children. Reinhardt was direct: "Parents are possessed of no constitutional right to prevent the public schools from providing information on that subject to their students in **any forum or manner** they select."

Consider the implications. By that reasoning, a school could conceivably bring in a dominatrix to describe the glories of S&M to first-graders and parents would have no recourse. But Reinhardt wasn't through. This incredible pinhead went on to write: "No such specific (parental) right can be found in the deep roots of the nation's history and tradition or implied in the concept of ordered liberty."

This kind of intellectual gibberish is part of the S-P manifesto, which even denies that, throughout American history, parents have traditionally had full discretion in matters of sexual disclosure to their children. Think about it: The S-Ps are now saying that the government should be allowed to introduce your kid to sexual matters even if you, the parent, object! Whatever the authorities choose, in whatever form, and in pursuit of whichever point of view is acceptable to the courts! Benjamin Franklin would have had these people **caned.**

Obviously, the Ninth Circuit Court of Appeals is firmly in the secular camp. You may remember that it was this very crew that ruled the words "under God" in the Pledge of Allegiance were un-Constitutional. That ruling, thank **God,** was thrown out and, indeed, the Ninth has been overturned about 75 percent of the time by the U.S. Supreme Court, according to **Cal Law,** California's legal news source. Even so, the fact that a powerful judicial body like this believes parents should have virtually no say in what their young children see and hear about sex in the public school system is beyond chilling.

Of course, parents who do not want their seven-year-olds asked if they "thought about having sex" were shocked. Their lawsuit against the school district was based on the belief that they had been "deprived of their right to control the upbringing of their children by introducing them to matters of and relating to sex in accordance with their personal and religious values and beliefs." Silly them, thinking parents have a right to bring up their own kids according to a specific belief system.

You will not be surprised to learn that the initial sex survey ruling propelled waves of joy throughout the S-P ranks. Parental authority had been radically diminished by a federal court, and as noted, that is a primary secular-progressive goal. Our S-P pal George Lakoff puts it bluntly: "Children are shaped by their **communities.**" The emphasis on the word "communities" is provided by Lakoff, himself, on page 90 of his **Elephant** book.

The S-P strategy with respect to children is not subtle. You can't achieve a brave new world without tearing down the bad old world. In order to change the thinking of America, you have to sweep out traditional Judeo-Christian values and replace them with radical secular-progressive values. If the public schools buy into the S-P agenda, which many of them do, then children will be exposed to another way of thinking apart from what their parents believe. Thus, the public schools have become a major battleground in the culture war, and hostilities are heating up.

Professor Lakoff has reinforced his S-P vision of education with this definition on how the government should set up the learning apparatus: "A vibrant, well-funded, and expanding public education system, with the highest standards for every child and school, where teachers nurture children's minds and often the children themselves, and where children are taught the truth about their nation—its wonders and its blemishes."

This pointed advice underscores my point: The S-P movement wants more authority for teachers and administrators and less for parents. Since most colleges are now firmly in the S-P camp, and colleges train the teachers of your children, just do the math. In addition (sorry), the secular-progressives are adamantly against vouchers for poor kids that would allow them the option of attending private schools. Why? Easy question. Most private schools would never even consider a sex survey for second-graders because that would be an intrusion on parental authority. In general, moreover, private schools pose a grave threat to the S-Ps because many of them reject secularism and teach traditional values. Public schools, however, are quite a different story. As mentioned, more and more of them are becoming S-P friendly.

It is fascinating, if a bit scary, to watch the S-P game plan to target American children in action. S-P indoctrination of kids is the goal, but the strategy is largely hidden behind the touchy-feely "nurturing" description of education. However, if you cut through all the bull, the key question is clear: If S-Ps are sincerely looking out for the kids, what is the secular-progressive philosophy on criminal justice, especially when children are directly affected? A brutal criminal case in Vermont and a civil lawsuit in Massachusetts shed some powerful light on that question.

At six years old, Susie (not her real name) was by all accounts an adorable child. Cute and generally nice to be around, Susie enjoyed the rural outdoor life in northern Vermont. But then, oddly, Susie began to change. She became withdrawn, sometimes sullen, and she didn't want to leave her house all that much. The innocent smiles of her toddler days became only a memory to those who knew her.

Susie lived with her uneducated mother and stepfather in a trailer home. Every Sunday, beginning when the girl was six years old, her mother's friend from high school, a laborer by the name of Mark Hulett, then thirty, would babysit for a few hours. This arrangement went on for about four years, until Susie was ten. And during that time, Hulett repeatedly raped the little girl.

Finally, Susie told her parents the story. Hulett was charged with a variety of sexual felonies and pled guilty. In a shocking statement, he explicitly told authorities what he had done to the little girl. I cannot recount what Hulett confessed to doing in these pages. The confession is simply too monstrous.

Presiding over the case was Judge Edward Cashman, a Vietnam vet with a rather eccentric sentencing record. In some cases, Cashman handed down tough penalties, but at other times he was inexplicably inappropriate. For example, the **Burlington Free Press** reported that he told a rape victim she had experienced "one of the harsh realities of life." After the young woman burst out crying, Cashman apologized. Onlookers in the courtroom were aghast.

As the confessed child rapist, Mark Hulett, stood before Judge Edward Cashman, some in the courtroom were expecting the criminal to get the maximum sentence: life. Instead, Cashman handed down a sentence of sixty days to ten years in state prison—and all but sixty **days** of the sentence was suspended. Why? So that the rapist could get "treatment" outside of prison. "The one message I want to get through is that anger doesn't solve anything," the judge explained. "It just corrodes your soul."

Susie's family was stunned. A man who had brutally and methodically violated an innocent child over a four-year period would be serving less time in prison than Martha Stewart had. How could this happen in America? Surely, the civil liberties groups, the press, and the public would not stand for it.

Vermont Judge Edward Cashman ignited a firestorm when he sentenced a convicted child rapist to a mere **sixty** days in jail.

Wrong. Most of the Vermont media, generally very liberal, actually **supported** the judge! In a shocking display of journalistic irresponsibility, the media portrayed him as a courageous man bent on reforming the justice system. Noah Hoffenburg, editorial director of the **Bennington Banner,** summarized the Vermont media position when he wrote: "We can see sexual predation as the disease itself; and make every attempt, as Judge Cashman did, to get to the source of the illness, thereby preventing the devastation of sexual assault in the future."

So, according to many in the Vermont media, child rape is an illness—not to be punished, but to be treated. Believe me, this kind of insane thinking is very, very common in the secular-progressive movement. In fact, there's even a name for it: "restorative justice."

During my investigation of Judge Cashman, I found that he actually taught a course on "restorative justice" at the National Judicial College, which advertises itself as "the nation's top judicial training institution." In other words, Cashman is a huge proponent of this madness, which encourages the legal system to find a way to "reintegrate offenders into society." The "restorative" crowd does not believe in retribution for crimes; they believe in "repairing harm" for both the victim and the offender. That is to say, society has a responsibility not only to the person who is harmed but also to the person **doing** the harm. Criminals need to be "nurtured." The S-Ps strike again.

Don't believe me? Well, guess who else has poured millions into getting "restorative justice" into the minds of those in the U.S. legal system? Does the name George Soros ring a bell?

Here's how bad this Vermont situation really was. Shortly after Judge Cashman sentenced the child rapist Hulett to sixty days, a man named Ralph Page ambled into the courtroom of another Vermont judge, Patricia Zimmerman. Page was there to answer charges that he had punched a woman in the face. Upon hearing the evidence against him, Page screamed at Judge Zimmerman: "That's f—— bull—." The judge promptly ruled Page in contempt of court and sentenced him to—you guessed it—sixty days in jail.

So there you have it. In Vermont you can get the same amount of jail time for systematically raping a little child over a four-year period as you can for cursing before a judge.

As for Judge Cashman, he remained defiantly steadfast. Before issuing his atrocious sentence, Cashman listened to the plea of the little girl's aunt, June Benway, who broke down sobbing in the courtroom while saying:

> The thought of my niece enduring years of sexual abuse sickens me. For four years she was a prisoner in her own home. For four years she had to fear going to bed at night.
>
> She's already developed behavioral problems that help to alienate herself from her peers. . . . When she is an adult, she won't be able to reminisce about her first kiss and experience the laughter and joy that should come with that memory. For her, the thought of her first kiss will probably evoke pain and anger. Her first kiss should not have been shared with some pervert. . . .

But Cashman was unmoved by the words of Ms. Benway. After she finished her statement, the judge began his explanation of the "justice" he was dispensing:

> I feel very strongly about retribution. And why? I didn't come to that easy. It isn't something that I started at. I started out as a just-dessert sentencer. I liked it. Cross the line, pop them. Then I discovered it accomplishes nothing of value. It doesn't make anything better.
>
> And I keep telling prosecutors, and they won't hear me, that punishment is

not enough. You can't be satisfied with punishment.

So in the mind of Vermont judge Edward Cashman, harshly punishing a child rapist is not the answer; "restorative justice" is. This abdication of common sense is truly shocking in a nation built on the bedrock concept of "equal justice for all" and "the punishment must fit the crime." But Vermont, it seems, has left the United States. Asked about Cashman's deplorable decision, retired Vermont chief justice Jeffrey Amestoy described Cashman as a "competent, caring, and conservative" trial judge.

Maybe in the Land of Oz, he would be.

Cashman's outrageous behavior, and the Vermont media's acceptance of it, made me furious. I was personally outraged and figured the national media would feel the same way I did. So I vigorously reported the story and asked the national press barons to get behind me and support the little girl and her family.

They didn't. Once again, I was the naïve culture warrior. Please call me Dopey Tzu. The network news organizations and CNN totally ignored the story, as did the major urban newspapers. Even though millions of Americans were deeply concerned and angered, the elite media passed.

Perhaps encouraged by the national media's apathy, some Vermont newspapers picked up the pace and actually began attacking me for my anti-Cashman stance: The **Brattleboro Reformer** called Cashman "One Tough Judge" in its headline and implied that I was a "demagogue."

The **Rutland Herald** editorialized: "Cashman issued the sentence precisely to protect children. It was the only way to provide Hulett the treatment he needs in a timely manner in order to deter him from committing a similar offense in the future."

Uh, the only way? I believe life in prison would deter Hulett from raping another child, would it not?

In fact, the only newspaper in Vermont to initially criticize Cashman was the **Burlington Free Press** (which also skewered me so it could have it both ways). But most Vermont media fell in with the S-P troops, a disgraceful exhibition that is not easy to digest. The plight of, and justice for, little Susie was obviously secondary to the "needs" of the rapist. And the Vermont media had no problem with that.

Yet the more I thought about the situation, the more it came to make sense. Vermont is the land of Howard Dean, who was five times elected governor. It is a state split between traditionalists and secular-progressives, with the

S-Ps obviously controlling much of the media. The public outcry in Vermont was also muted. To be sure, thousands of Vermonters were angry, but many of them told **Factor** producers they were afraid to stand up for fear of criticism. Everyone agreed there is a powerful and intimidating S-P presence in the state of Vermont.

But the **Factor** culture warriors wouldn't let go. My staff and I pounded the story night after night, with revelations about Vermont's weak leaders and chaotic legislature. Thousands of Americans besieged the Vermont governor with e-mails. Finally, the state wobbled. Judge Cashman, realizing his career was sliding down the drain, issued a new sentence for the child rapist Hulett: three to ten years. And Hulett would get "treatment" in the Big House.

This case is one of the most vivid examples of the culture war ever on display. A guy rapes a little girl over a four-year period and it takes an intensely fought national battle just to see he spends three years in prison. Most legal experts in Vermont believe he'll be paroled after doing the minimum.

There is no question the little girl's human rights were violated. But not one person from the S-P groups Human Rights Watch, the ACLU, or the National Organization for Women stepped

up to protect her. Likewise, liberal Vermont politicians, who are supposedly looking out for the downtrodden, like Senators Jeffords and Leahy, Governor Dean, and Congressman Bernie Sanders, said not a word. All the S-P warriors sat it out. And that's a fact.

Now, the logical question is: Why would the S-P movement want to stand behind an insane sentence for a child rapist? What's in it for them?

Well, we've explored the "restorative justice" link, but there's also something else. In the S-P world, few judgments are made about personal behavior; the old "if it feels good, do it" adage from the sixties is commonly accepted. But, usually, even the ACLU draws the line at violent criminal behavior. However, the restorative justice concept is picking up steam in the S-P ranks—the "disease" excuse is featured prominently in S-P criminal philosophy. We shouldn't prosecute street-level dope dealers, for example, we should give them "treatment," because substance abuse is a disease that needs to be cured, not punished. And it is the "illness," not the person, that is the cause of the harm people might do. It's really not their fault, you see. In the words of Judge Edward Cashman: "Punishment is not the answer."

Many of us would like to kill a person who raped our child. That is a natural reaction, a genuine emotional response to a crime that is so heinous it is off the chart. But in the brave new world of the S-P movement, even child rape is not enough to condemn the criminal to spend much of his or her life behind bars. Even though the child is devastated for life, the criminal must be "healed" in order for true justice to take place. This is what America will come to if the secular-progressives ever take over—and if you think I'm exaggerating, you're wrong. The states of Minnesota and Vermont have been heavily influenced by secular-progressive thought. It is no accident that those two states are the only ones in the Union that officially sanction the philosophy of "restorative justice."

The final part of this miserable story deals with our pals at the **New York Times,** the "all the news that's fit to print" newspaper. Apparently, the plight of the little Vermont girl was not "fit to print," because the **Times** totally ignored the story. Now, I thought that rather strange. You'll remember the vicious attack on me by **Times** columnist Nicholas Kristof over the Christmas controversy. Kristof, the human rights guy, described me as akin to a Muslim fundamentalist. He also challenged me to join him in reporting human rights abuses abroad.

Well, here's my question: If Africa is in play, Nick, why not Vermont?

So on February, 3, 2006, I dedicated my syndicated newspaper column to Kristof and his employers at the **Times** and wrote this:

> Here's an update on that young Vermont girl whose life has been made a living hell by a justice system that literally could not care less about her.
>
> You may remember that 34-year-old Mark Hulett pleaded guilty to raping the child over a four-year period, starting when she was just six-years-old. The judge in the case frowned when he heard the confession and promptly sentenced the vicious criminal to **60 days** in prison. A few journalists, including myself, picked up on the outrage and, under enormous pressure, Judge Edward Cashman changed the sentence to three years; still an incredible miscarriage of justice.
>
> The girl, now 10, is being raised by foster parents. Vermont authorities believe her mother and stepfather are incapable of properly protecting the child. She is undergoing counseling and is in school, but, according to those who see her every day, she's confused and unhappy.

Surely this young girl's human rights have been violated; no person on this earth should have to suffer the way she has.

A few weeks ago, **New York Times** columnist Nicholas Kristof criticized me for reporting on the Christmas controversy. Kristof asserted that I fabricated the story and ignored "real" stories like the suffering in the Sudan.

Kristof wrote: "So I have a challenge for Mr. O'Reilly: If you really want to defend traditional values, then come with me on a trip to Darfur. I'll introduce you to mothers who have had their babies clubbed to death in front of them, to teenage girls who have been gang-raped . . ."

Now, I do three hours of daily news analysis on TV and radio; there's no way I can go to Africa in light of those commitments. However, I'm glad Kristof can go because somebody needs to spotlight that terrible situation.

But an interesting thing happened shortly after that Kristof column: the 60-day sentence for the child rapist came to light. Because Kristof had referenced teenage rape in his criticism of me, I fully expected to see him and **The New York Times** all over the Vermont situation. After all, this human rights violation happened just a few hundred miles north of New York City.

But the **Times** didn't cover the Vermont story—didn't even mention it. And there was not a word from my pal Nicholas Kristof, the human rights guy.

So what's going on here? Aren't liberal press advocates champions of the downtrodden? Maybe Kristof can write another column explaining to me why the Vermont child doesn't matter to him or his newspaper.

I hope this doesn't sound bitter, because I don't mean it to be. I am genuinely perplexed by the sanctimonious left-wing press, which doesn't consider a 60-day jail term for a child rapist an outrage.

While the **Times** rails against alleged human-rights violations in Guantanamo Bay and other far-off places, it apparently has no interest in protecting poor American children from predators and irresponsible judges.

Something isn't right here. What say you on the left?

Now, that column was written with the intention of embarrassing Kristof and the **New York Times.** I admit it. Remember, that newspaper is the secular-progressive Bible. My feeling is that the **Times** ignored the Vermont story because I was so involved in it and because the **Times** is definitely on board with the "restorative justice" movement. But I could be wrong.

For the record, about a week after I wrote that column calling the **Times** out for ignoring the little girl in Vermont, Nicholas Kristof wrote another column asking his readers to send money so a ticket could be purchased in order to send me to Africa. It was a dopey article, the point of which escaped just about everyone I know. But Kristof did comment on my crusading for justice in Vermont. He called it "good stuff."

Well, thanks, Nick, but I'm still waiting for your employers to assign someone to expose the myriad of human rights violations going on inside the United States. It would be great for the powerful **New York Times** to get behind Jessica's Law, a tough anti–sexual predator law being adopted by states across the country, wouldn't it?

Never gonna happen.

And the atrocities keep on coming in the USA. Soon after the Vermont debacle, an Ohio judge named John Connor pronounced sentence on a man who forced a five-year-old boy and an eleven-year-old boy to have sex with him. The man admitted committing the felonies and to doing a number of other horrendous things to these children. Connor could have sentenced the predator to ten years in prison. But he did not. He gave the degenerate **probation.** No prison time at all. Connor pronounced that the man had a "disease."

I let Judge Connor have it on **The Factor,** arguing that the state had to impeach him. Even after the Vermont experience, I thought the Ohio press would be on my side. The **Toledo Blade** was. But most of the other media condemned me. Newspapers in Cincinnati, Akron, and Dayton actually supported Connor. It was another shocking display of media irresponsibility. The **Dayton Daily News** was the worst. It leveled personal attacks on me, the governor of Ohio, and the attorney general of the state for demanding Connor's removal. It was, perhaps, the most despicable thing I have ever seen in an American newspaper. And, no surprise, the Dayton paper is a bastion of secular-progressive opinion.

Taking the evidence presented, I believe it is fair to say that not only does the S-P movement sympathize with child predators because of their "disease"; they are also making it easier for these criminals to operate. To prove this, we must travel to the Commonwealth of Massachusetts, a reliable stronghold of secular-progressive thought.

Earlier in this book, I mentioned that the ACLU is representing the North American Man-Boy Love Association in a civil lawsuit. That case, I argued, proves that the ACLU is not only misguided, it is dangerous. Here are some more details that, I hope, prove this point once and for all. We begin with the fact that the ACLU believes NAMBLA's "rights" are being violated. So please consider that the starting point of this terrible situation.

On October 1, 1997, ten-year-old Jeffrey Curley was playing in the front yard of his Cambridge, Massachusetts, home. A few yards away, two men, Salvatore Sicari and Charles Jaynes, were watching Jeffrey from their parked car.

Sicari and Jaynes talked it over—could they kidnap the boy and get away unseen? It was risky in broad daylight, but the men, losers both, decided to try. Leaping out of the car, they grabbed the boy, threw him inside, and sped off. But Jeffrey fought back hard. Finally, the men suffocated the boy with a gasoline-soaked rag and drove to Jaynes's apartment, where they sexually abused Jeffrey's body. Afterward, they drove to Maine, where they dumped the young boy's corpse into a river. It does not get worse than this.

Massachusetts detectives did a great job on the case, and both Sicari and Jaynes received life in prison. During court testimony, Jaynes's diary was introduced. In said diary was a description of the NAMBLA Web site and Jaynes's writing that it encouraged him to act out his violent fantasies on young boys. As I told you earlier, Jaynes accessed the NAMBLA Web site at the Boston Public Library. Remember, the ACLU and S-P movement want no restrictions on library Internet access.

Not surprisingly, Jeffrey Curley's family was so appalled by the NAMBLA connection that they filed a $200 million federal lawsuit against the group, seeking to put it out of business once and for all. It fell to the Curley family to attempt to do what the U.S. justice system has been unable to do—crush NAMBLA.

By the way, it is worth noting that one of the most popular NAMBLA publications is titled "The Survival Manual: The Man's Guide to Staying Alive in Man-Boy Sexual Relationships." This revolting "manual" explains how to insinuate yourself into a child's life and get away with molesting the boy. Sick doesn't even begin to cover it.

After the Curley family filed its suit, it was answered—by the ACLU. The S-P shock troops took the case to "protect" the free-speech rights of NAMBLA. ACLU Massachusetts legal director John Reinstein said in a press release: "Regardless to whether people agree with or abhor NAMBLA's views, holding the organization responsible for crimes committed by others who read their material would gravely endanger important first amendment freedoms."

Once again, a theoretical argument is put forth to defend active evil. As with the war on terror, the S-P vanguard cannot come to grips with the fact that NAMBLA has no place in any civilized society, is an organization that appears to be criminal, encouraging child rape, and should be put out of business any legal way possible. But in the "anything goes" world of the secular-progressives, theory is much more important than protecting the kids.

One more item to bolster my argument: the ACLU's war against the Boy Scouts has received a lot of attention. Very simply, the Scouts decline to approve openly gay Scoutmasters and require that the boys acknowledge a "higher power." The ACLU sees this as a violation of gay and atheist rights, even though the Supreme Court has ruled that the Scouts and all other private organizations have the right to make their own charters and rules.

So, all over the country, the ACLU has sued the Boy Scouts, seeking to have them denied public assistance and access, such as having a jamboree on city property. It is a jihad against the Scouts, no question. Once again doing the math, I have come up with this equation: NAMBLA gets ACLU support. The Boy Scouts get ACLU attacks. Am I wrong here?

Finally, let's go back to school, where the S-P assault on American children is being intensely waged under the guise of looking out for the kids. Besides abortion, the one issue that will drive any secular-progressive crazy is school "vouchers" for disadvantaged children.

Because so many public schools are ineptly run and even dangerous to attend, states like Florida have provided assistance to poor families who wish to send their children to private schools. In the high school where I taught in the 1970s—Monsignor Edward Pace in Opa Locka, Florida—forty low-income students were receiving tuition assistance from the state. But the S-P Florida Supreme Court—you remember, the one that ruled in favor of Al Gore in the 2000 election and was overturned by the Supreme Court—decided that Florida violated its constitution by directing fees to private schools. Predictably, the court rationalized its ruling by invoking the separation of church and state theory. But in the real world, where most of us have to live, many of the poor children involved were forced to return to violent, chaotic public schools.

The secular-progressives will tell you they are looking out for your "rights" and the overall welfare of children in the school voucher debate. But that's an impossible argument to win when you realize that a poor kid doesn't have the same "rights" as a rich kid to attend a school their parents choose. This is flat-out classism and a stark denial of equal opportunity.

But, as we've learned, the true S-P agenda wants nothing to do with the traditional Judeo-Christian values that are taught in most private schools. That is really the issue here. The separation of church and state argument is just a ruse, and there's proof. After World War II, more than 2 million veterans were given educational "vouchers" paid for by the government in order to afford to attend the college of their choice. Many of those vets chose religious colleges. Back then, the S-P movement was in its infancy and little was said.

But over the years, as the S-P forces in America grew in strength, the opposition to all government assistance involving any religious affiliation intensified. It came to a head in a 1999 lawsuit involving educational assistance to the poor in Cleveland. In that case, the Supreme Court ruled that as long as the government didn't **force** an American student to attend a religious school, there was nothing unConstitutional about supplying poor American families with money to attend any school of their "choice."

This entire issue, of course, is about free choice and the Constitutional right to pursue happiness on an equal basis. Using a variety of studies, ABC newsman John Stossel has documented that poor kids who use vouchers to attend private schools dramatically improve their academic performance. So the intense S-P opposition to school vouchers isn't exactly "nurturing" poor children, now is it?

Want more evidence that S-P opposition to school vouchers damages kids? Try this: In Washington, D.C., according to the National Center for Education Statistics, public school spending on each pupil is now over $10,000 per child per year, an astounding amount and about double what it was thirty years ago. D.C. Catholic schools spend far less per pupil than the public schools do. And—you guessed it—test scores for the Catholic school kids are far higher than those for the public school students. In fact, 98 percent of kids graduating from D.C. Catholic schools go on to college, while almost 40 percent of D.C. public school students never graduate from high school; they drop out. Once again, the math tells the story. Too bad so many public school kids will never learn how to do math.

The sad truth is there are few public schools in the United States that can compete with private schools because of the discipline factor. Private schools work intensely with parents and demand that strict academic and behavioral guidelines be followed. In many public schools, "self-esteem" is the lesson of the day, and social promotion the school fight song.

And once a kid gets to college, well, forget about hearing the traditional point of view very much. Most American universities have become secular-progressive theme parks. Even once-traditional schools like Georgetown and Villanova have suffered a large infusion of S-P influence.

In fact, a study by the Higher Education Research Institute at UCLA surveyed more than fifty-five thousand college professors about their political beliefs. Asked to describe themselves ideologically, 48 percent said they were "liberal" or "far left," 18 percent said "conservative" or "far right," and 34 percent described themselves as "middle of the road."

But wait a minute. What exactly does "middle of the road" mean on America's college campuses? It is impossible to nail down completely, but let me offer this insight: In the mid-nineties, as I mentioned, I attended Harvard's Kennedy School of Government. I learned a lot there and am proud of earning a master's degree in public administration with decent grades.

Press and media studies at the Kennedy School are done in the Shorenstein Center, which is headed up by former **New York Times** reporter Alex Jones, a committed liberal. But Professor Jones does not see himself that way. He believes he's a fair and balanced guy and said so on **The O'Reilly Factor.** He also said the **New York Times** is not a liberal newspaper and the former editor of the **Los Angeles Times,** Jon Carroll, whom Jones hired to teach at the Kennedy School, is not a liberal guy either.

I thought that analysis fascinating, because while at the **L.A. Times,** Mr. Carroll hired far-left bomb-thrower Michael Kinsley to run the editorial page, which also featured radical S-P icon columnists like Robert Scheer. Under Carroll, the **Times** lurched to the left, and drastically declined in circulation. Maybe that was a coincidence, but Carroll eventually quit. Soon after his departure, Kinsley and Scheer were fired by the Tribune Company, which owns the **L.A. Times.**

Now, I could be wrong (have I said that before?). I mean, maybe Jones, Carroll, Kinsley, and Scheer are all "middle of the road." I can only go by what they've written and what they've said. I can't read their minds.

Professor Jones, I believe, sincerely thinks he's a nonpartisan educator. Again, maybe he is. The point here is that in academic circles "middle of the road" is completely different from what it would be in, say, Tupelo, Mississippi. I believe it is safe to assume that on most college campuses in the United States, S-P thought rules, at least in public.

Nowhere is that point better illustrated than at the University of Colorado. This is the home of radical professor Ward Churchill, the unhinged "ethnic studies" professor who proudly proclaimed that many of the Americans killed on 9/11 were "little Eichmanns" who deserved their fate because they were evil capitalists. You remember the outcry over that.

Well, despite all the controversy and serious questions about Churchill's background and scholarship, he emerged as a hero among many in the secular-progressive community. But he's not a hero to me.

So when I heard that Hamilton College in upstate New York had hired Churchill to speak on campus, I really let the college have it on radio and TV. Why pay this guy money to spew that kind of hate? I asked. Doesn't anyone care that his vile words bring pain to the families who lost people in the World Trade Center attack? Would Hamilton be hiring David Duke to speak anytime soon?

Hamilton folded. Churchill did not speak.

As soon as the decision to throw this loon overboard was made, the S-P media sprang into action. It was the usual bilge: O'Reilly's a fascist, a bully, a terrible human being in every way. Secular-progressive columnist Richard Cohen, who writes for the **Washington Post**, was distraught over the Churchill situation:

> Then Bill O'Reilly struck. The Fox TV commentator went to town on the controversy, finding the usual liberal idiocy at the usual liberal college perpetuated by the usual liberal morons. Having rounded up his usual suspects, O'Reilly ended a segment about Hamilton by providing the name of the college's president, Joan Hinde Stewart, her e-mail address and the school's phone number.

Then, blood dripping from his evil heart, he asked his deranged viewers to "keep your comments respectable." The school caved.

Now, Richard Cohen is one of the most fanatical S-P media people working today. He truly hates me and obviously despises the "deranged" millions all over the world who watch **The Factor.** Of course, I couldn't care less, and I don't hate him. In fact, the only thing about Cohen that even registered on my radar is that he often used personal attacks in his column to smear those with whom he disagreed.

But, I'm pleased to say, Richard Cohen no longer does that very much. After I gently advised him on the air to cease and desist from the smear tactics, he did. Good for him.

However, Cohen's decision may have had something to do with karma. In May 2006 he wrote in the **Washington Post** that television satirist Stephen Colbert had bombed while doing a monologue at the Washington White House Correspondents dinner. Immediately Cohen was barraged by hundreds of hateful e-mails. Apparently two far-left smear Web sites had urged their readers to attack Cohen. The writer called the chorus a "digital lynch mob": "It seemed that most of my correspondents had been egged on to attack me by various blogs. . . . All in all, I was—I am, and I guess I remain—the worthy object of ignorant, false and downright idiotic vituperation."

I know how you feel there, Richard. What I don't understand is why this is news to you. As the aforementioned NPR ombudsman Jeffrey Dvorkin wrote about the vile Web sites Media Matters and Think Progress: "[They] encourage people to express strong feelings; the level of pure acrimony seemed to me to rise to the level of hate speech."

Even the ombudsman for NPR knows the score.

Summing up, there is no question that the S-P movement is firmly entrenched on most college campuses and is making a lot of progress in public secondary and grammar schools. That is worrisome. The educational battlefield is a key area in the culture war. Here, especially, traditional forces are on the defensive and are heavily outnumbered. Right now American voters renounce secular-progressive initiatives again and again. But will that hold twenty years from today?

That, for the traditional warrior, is the key question.

Ten

The Color of Tradition

What's goin' on?

—MARVIN GAYE

A friend of mine spied an African American woman reading one of my books on an Amtrak train and, smiling, brought it to my attention. He thought it was great but was a bit surprised. He should not have been. Many African Americans are deeply traditional, though they might vote Democratic or even be liberal thinkers.

Dr. Martin Luther King Jr. was a traditionalist. In almost every public statement he made, he called upon God to inspire him and deliver justice. In his **Letter from a Birmingham Jail**, he wrote: "[Civil rights protesters stand for] the most sacred values in our Judeo-Christian heritage, thereby carrying our whole nation back to those great wells of democracy."

Did I read that right? "Our Judeo-Christian heritage"? Of course, Dr. King understood that to mean the traditional tenets of freedom for all, justice for all, and generosity of spirit and with material things. Martin Luther King Jr.'s words are more important than ever, because the S-P movement not only scorns Judeo-Christian philosophy, some of its members even deny America has a heritage based on that philosophy.

Bill Cosby is also a traditionalist. He travels the country urging black Americans to return to the American traditions of self-discipline, self-reliance, and self-respect. Cosby understands that moral relativism is not helping black Americans overcome their historical disadvantages. The key to success, as Cosby well knows, is a strong traditional education and hard work.

And, surprise, the Reverend Jesse Jackson is a traditionalist, at least in some ways. The proof came when he sided with Terri Schiavo's family in the controversy over whether the Florida woman should be removed from life support. Jackson opined that any mistake made in the emotional case should be made on the side of life. The S-Ps must have hated that.

Once again, not all liberals are secular-progressives, and not all Democrats approve of the S-P vision. And that is certainly true with the African American community.

Although 89 percent of blacks voted Democratic in 2004, when it comes to social issues African Americans are largely in the traditional camp. A Pew Research Center poll taken in July 2005 found that 75 percent of black Americans believe secular-progressives push too far in keeping religion out of schools and government. Only 17 percent of African American voters want to legalize gay marriage—an overwhelming statement of traditionalist conviction.

Those attitudes, strongly held, are a disaster for the S-P movement, which is why you rarely see any blacks associated with it. The ACLU is almost entirely white, as is Air America, as is the George Clooney S-P crew in Hollywood.

George Soros and Peter Lewis, the big S-P moneymen, travel in almost exclusively white circles. Bill Moyers and his media followers are all a whiter shade of pale, to quote an old Procol Harum rock song.

Because the African American political establishment is largely locked into one issue—advancement of blacks through government largesse—African Americans remain largely on the sidelines in the culture war. Generally speaking, taking up the battle is simply not relevant to them, because traditionalists have not defined the culture war to coincide with their interests. I believe that is a huge mistake.

In many black communities, Christian churches are prominent centerpieces. Faith is an important tradition in black America. That's why the gay marriage issue is overwhelmingly rejected by blacks. Their religion says homosexuality is not acceptable, and many African Americans bitterly resent the argument that marriage for homosexuals is a civil right. If you want a lively discussion, walk into a black church and put that on the table.

So there is no solace or future for the S-Ps in the black precincts. Take another issue: drugs. Many African Americans have seen firsthand what narcotics can do; they don't want hard drugs legalized. Lawlessness and the breakdown of the traditional family in poor black neighborhoods (the out-of-wedlock birth rate for blacks is 70 percent) has deepened the cycle of poverty and deprivation. Any sane person can see that.

And older African Americans generally deplore the rise of gangsta rap and the disintegration of civility among some young black people. This is a big Cosby theme, and he pounds it home in his lectures again and again, despite attacks on him by the S-P community, which often views the hate-filled rap lyrics as "genuine expression."

And Cosby is not alone. Oprah Winfrey has just about banned street rappers from her program. The despicable Ludacris complained that Oprah simply ignored him when he appeared on her program with the cast of a movie in which he appeared. Oprah clearly understands the damage "gangsta rap" has done and is not about to embrace the pushers of it.

The culture war question is: Why are so many prominent African Americans opposed to the secular-progressive viewpoint when S-P principals like Susan Sarandon and George Clooney

Two contrasting faces of African American culture: the civil rights hero Martin Luther King Jr., and the ludicrous rapper Ludacris.

would do just about anything in order to secure "black" approval? The answer to that question lies in the S-P mantra of "no judgments" about most personal behavior.

Writing in the **New York Times**, Harvard professor Orlando Patterson, a respected African American thinker, put forth some research:

> So why were [young blacks] flunking out [of high school]? Their candid answer was that what sociologists call the "cool-pose culture" of young black men was simply too gratifying to give up. For these young men, it was almost like a drug, hanging out on the street after school, shopping and dressing sharply, sexual conquests, party drugs, hip-hop music and culture, the fact that almost all the superstar athletes and a great many of the nation's best entertainers were black.
>
> Not only was living this subculture immensely fulfilling, the boys said, it also brought them a great deal of respect from white youths. . . . Sadly, their complete engagement in this part of the American culture mainstream, which they created and which feeds their pride and self-respect, is a major factor in their disconnection from the socioeconomic mainstream.

Many traditionalists, of course, deplore what is happening with some black young people. They rightfully condemn the incredibly selfish behavior that promotes the use and abuse of other people under the false banner of "oppression." But the S-P crowd, especially the mainstream media, has glorified the gangsta world and, indeed, makes money from it. Those white, middle-aged, ponytailed music executives are no better than crack dealers. They know their product dehumanizes its constant customer and encourages awful behavior. But the bank run is all that matters. And alert African Americans understand the exploitation that is going on. Bill Cosby and Oprah speak for them.

The upshot of all this is that it's safe to say few, if any, citizens are enlisting in the S-P corps in East St. Louis or South Central Los Angeles. But, again, not many blacks are waving the traditional flag, either. It would take a strong black leader who understands that the Judeo-Christian tradition, as well as a return to discipline and personal accountability, would greatly aid the advancement of African Americans. Until such a leader arrives, most black Americans will remain disengaged from the culture war that is raging around them. And that's a shame.

Eleven

Close Encounters of the Secular Kind

Keep your friends close, but your enemies closer.

—DON CORLEONE

By now, you might have ascertained that I have a myriad of enemies. In fact, I probably have more myriads than just about anybody in America with the exception of President Bush and the Clintons. I mean, lots of people really, **really** despise me. I believe it's kind of a love-hate thing; that is, they **love** to loathe me. Some of those far-left Web sites, for example, might evaporate if they couldn't defame me on a daily basis.

As I said earlier, all of that means nothing to me unless these people try to cause harm. Then I do care. Enough to strike back fast and hard. I am definitely not Gandhi (another traditionalist, by the way).

What I am about to say might sound delusional, but I believe the genesis of the O'Reilly loathing lies in the fact that I win most of my battles in the culture war. If you've watched me on the tube over the years, you've seen me right a number of obvious wrongs, and expose more than a few bad guys. I've mentioned some of those stories in this book, but there are scores of others. From nailing the Florida judge who allowed eleven-year-old Carlie Bruscha's killer to avoid jail on a parole violation and walk the streets free to kill Carlie, to holding the Pepsi Company responsible for hiring the vile rapper Ludacris to promote its products, to encouraging CBS not to run a movie that unnecessarily demeaned Ronald and Nancy Reagan—we have accomplished much in the culture war. And that, of course, drives the S-P forces nuts.

Most of the time, the secular-progressive players avoid me. George Soros would never consent to appear on **The Factor;** nor would Bill Moyers or Peter Lewis or Walter Cronkite. They are the S-P archers. They aim their arrows toward traditionalists and let fly, all the while keeping their distance from the counterattack of debate.

But there have been exceptions, occasions when some S-P principals did get up close and personal with me. What follows are some of those situations.

George Clooney: More of a far-left ideologue than an enlisted S-P culture warrior, the actor nevertheless consistently toes the secular-progressive line and is up front in doing so. Clooney is an outspoken liberal activist who likes to involve himself in current events. You may remember he was one of the organizers of a telethon designed to raise money for the families devastated by the attack on 9/11, and that situation brought him into a collision course with me.

This is old territory for some of you, but a quick recap is needed to set up what has become an ongoing "situation." On September 21, 2001, Clooney and scores of other stars appeared in a telethon titled "America: A Tribute to Heroes." All the publicity and the actual TV pitches made clear that the funds raised by this telethon were to be used to help the 9/11 families. The celebrities donated their time (and sometimes money), and the folks responded with enormous generosity. Reportedly, something like $266 million was raised by that one event. The money was turned over primarily to the United Way, but other charities benefited as well. On the surface, everything looked fine; a job well done.

But it quickly became apparent that some serious problems had developed in the aftermath of the telethon. In the area of Long Island, New York, where I live, at least thirty families lost

George Clooney and I are two Irishmen who see the world differently.

loved ones in the 9/11 al-Qaeda attack. This wasn't "tape at eleven"; this was real life. It was just heartbreaking to see the pain and confusion of little kids who had no idea why Daddy or Mommy didn't come home. I still see these children nearly every day. 9/11 is **real** personal for me.

Thus, when some 9/11 family members in my town approached me a couple of months after the celebrity telethon saying they had heard nothing from the United Way and asking if I could get them information, of course I said yes. I quickly assigned a couple of **Factor** investigators to call the United Way, the Red Cross, and all the other charities involved in helping the families. At first we just wanted to know what was going on. What we found was utter chaos.

Most of the organizations that received donated telethon funds had no databases containing information about the 9/11 families and no way to directly answer questions from them; the charities themselves were completely on the defensive about any disbursement of the money. In fact, the Red Cross told us it wouldn't even give much of the donated funds to the families; it had, without telling the public, unilaterally decided to put aside millions of 9/11 dollars for future disasters.

After I began reporting the story, outrage grew and the Red Cross quickly reversed itself—pledging all the money would go to the families. The Red Cross board of directors also replaced its CEO. But, to my amazement, the United Way continued to stonewall. So, after carefully thinking the situation over, I made a direct appeal to the stars who had worked the telethon: Please ask the United Way to be more forthcoming.

Incredibly, out of the scores of celebrities who asked for your money on TV, only four stepped up and agreed they had a responsibility to ask the United Way to be more responsive: Clint Eastwood, Kurt Russell, Goldie Hawn, and the singer James Brown. That was it. The rest of them went to ground. Except, that is, for George Clooney. He went on the attack.

Clooney's press agent, a guy named Stan Rosenfield, began bad-mouthing me and Fox News around Hollywood and then issued a press release in which Clooney compared me to Senator Joseph McCarthy and stated: "[O'Reilly's] accusation that the fund is being mishandled and misused is nothing short of a lie. The money is going to the right people. And to make certain of this, the United Way is taking some time [to distribute it] . . ."

Clooney then went on the Letterman program and said I made up the entire story—a kind of forerunner to the strategy the S-Ps used during the Christmas controversy.

We, of course, invited Clooney on **The Factor** to talk things over; I wasn't angry with him at first, I just thought he was stunningly misinformed. As I wrote in my previous book—**Who's Looking Out for You?**—all I wanted Clooney and the other celebrities to do was ask the United Way to communicate directly with the families. Apparently, that benign and reasonable request upset many stars. Guys like Tom Hanks claimed I was interested in the story solely for "ratings." Julia Roberts also said something to that effect. But it was Clooney who was the most adamant—I was Satan!

I must say the whole thing was incredibly stupid. Did George Clooney not see all the family members we brought on **The Factor** who said they could not get any of their questions answered by the United Way? Did he not notice that the director of the Bergen County, New Jersey, branch of the United Way described the

entire 9/11 donation program as chaotic? I mean, come on, transcripts are available for all my programs, the facts were readily accessible. All George Clooney and his publicist had to do was take legendary baseball manager Casey Stengel's advice and "look it up."

But it soon became clear to me that, for George Clooney, this was not about the 9/11 families. No, this was about something else. Behind his blustery indignation, what was really in play was Clooney's ego and his intense personal dislike of me. Remember, he is a far-left guy. So even after the National Academy of Television Arts and Sciences acknowledged **The Factor**'s entire 9/11 reporting with a special citation, Clooney continued his bizarre stance. I chalked it up to unchecked narcissism and put Clooney's nonsense on the shelf.

About four years later, in October 2005, the George Clooney/O'Reilly saga took a surprise turn. A major New York City publicist invited me to attend a private screening of Clooney's movie **Good Night and Good Luck.** The film, based on the life of legendary television journalist Edward R. Murrow, was to open a few weeks later, and I was eager to see it. But the invitation made me wary. Obviously, George Clooney was no friend of mine or of my brand of journalism; why would he want to give me a preview of his film?

The invitation stated that the screening was to be followed by a dinner hosted by Clooney and Walter Cronkite (surprise), but no way was I going to that. Generally, I try to avoid those kinds of things unless friends of mine are involved or money is being raised for charity. This culture warrior is not good at small talk and is also usually a tired guy by the end of the day. So the dinner was out, but I did want to see the movie.

After thinking it over, I decided to take a bodyguard, **Factor** executive producer Dave Tabacoff, and attend the screening. The small theater was packed with people like Dan Rather, Mike Wallace, and Andy Rooney, already a kind of establishment blessing for the enterprise. And the film turned out to be good; Clooney had done excellent work.

When the lights went up, I left the theater—and guess who I bumped into in the lobby? Hi, there, George, you ol' rascal.

Sensing drama, the exiting crowd hushed and stared as I walked over to the actor. He's about 5′10″, so he had to look up to all 6′4″ of me. I shook his hand and told him the film was excellent. I even invited him on **The Factor** if he wanted to publicize the movie. I said we'd drop all the other stuff and focus on the film. I suggested the past was the past. I tried to be concil-

iatory without being obsequious, and it wasn't difficult because, again, I have nothing personally against George Clooney.

Probably employing his acting skills, Clooney shook my hand in return and was convincingly pleasant. Meanwhile, his oily publicist, Stan Rosenfield, hovered close behind him. The entire chat took maybe forty-five seconds. I then congratulated David Strathairn, the actor who played Edward R. Murrow, and went home.

Now, I didn't really expect to hear from Clooney about my invitation, but I didn't expect anything negative either. Wrong again, dense culture warrior! The very next day, Clooney launched a series of nasty personal attacks against me in the **Washington Post,** the **New York Daily News,** and a few other places. I was surprised. I had been stupid (again).

So let's recap. Clooney looks me in the eye and cordially shakes my hand while I politely compliment his movie and invite him to promote it on my program. Then, when I'm not around, he smears me to the press. That is exactly what George Clooney did. He's quite a guy.

One footnote: Clooney's display was so over-the-top classless, it made me curious. What kind of person behaves like that? So I called a high-ranking Hollywood person I know—let's call him "Deep Boxoffice," or D.B.

After I related to D.B. the exact story I just told you, D.B. laughed and said he knew all about the situation. In his view, Rosenfield and Clooney hoped that attacking me in the press would cause me to hit back on TV and a public brawl would ensue. They were using the Franken tactic: Get free publicity by goading O'Reilly into a media fight. **Good Night and Good Luck** did not have much of a publicity budget, and a national controversy flamed by a partisan media would likely gain attention and thus sell tickets.

But this time, I didn't play. However, I did allow Clooney to get close, proving that even after the Franken episode, I had not completely learned my lesson. Some of these S-P people are beyond shameless. They do not operate like regular folks. Luckily, I seethed privately about the Clooney assault but did not make it a public matter. So I am getting there. With some culture warriors, it is a long process.

Michael Moore: The clown prince of the secular-progressive movement, Moore, like George Clooney, is a talented filmmaker. Also like Clooney, Moore's primary interest lies in the political area, but he does aggressively advance the S-P cause in almost all his projects. Moore is especially popular in secular-progressive Europe, where his anti-American posture is widely acclaimed. In his travels abroad, he frequently claims that most Americans are dopes and U.S. leadership is a tool of the corrupt, unfeeling big corporations.

Moore made his reputation attacking General Motors in a film called **Roger and Me.** He espouses a fuzzy type of socialism where workers should be "nurtured" and big corporations should be kicked to the curb. In keeping with his message, Moore's public image is that of a working guy not much interested in material things. Typically unshaven and wearing a cheap cap, Moore presents himself as a working-class hero. But the truth is much different.

Like many S-P showbiz types, Moore enjoys his wealth and comfort. According to reporting done by Peter Schweizer in his book **Do as I Say (Not as I Do)**, Moore owns two lavish homes, holds stock in some of the corporations he claims to despise, and, in 2003,

Michael Moore, the clown prince of the secular-progressive movement.

just before he'd hit it big with his anti-Bush movie, switched his primary residence from New York to Michigan, thereby saving himself a bundle on income taxes.

And do you know what? I don't care. Moore can do whatever he wants with his money; that's no concern of mine. Everyone has inconsistencies in his or her life. If you think Moore is a phony, you may be right. But on the culture war battlefield, that is not what really counts.

That's because Michael Moore has terminally marginalized himself. He now preaches solely to a far-left, devoutly S-P choir. His outrageous assertions after 9/11 were largely discredited by reasonable people on all sides. For instance, that the Bush family intervened to protect questionable Saudis in the days after the attack. Check out his Web site and you might agree that the man has blasted off into outer space. Moore used to be entertaining, and once in a while he actually made some good points. But somewhere between the moon and New York City, as Christopher Cross once sang, Moore became a bitter anti-American extremist. As a further sign of decline, he now routinely attacks people personally. There's a niche market for that kind of thing, but little more (sorry).

Before 9/11, I enjoyed having Michael Moore on **The Factor**; he was funny without being mean-spirited. But the last time we sparred, it was a different experience, a sad disappointment.

Since Moore had been accessible to **The Factor** in the past, we were surprised when he ducked us while promoting **Fahrenheit 9/11**, his hate-Bush movie. His publicist simply would not confirm any appearance with us. But while Moore can run, anyone who dresses like that can't hide. In July 2004, I spotted Moore on the street outside of the Fleet Center in Boston, where the Democratic Convention was in progress.

I jumped out of my car and yelled: "Hey, Moore! You're ducking me."

Luckily, a cameraman from the Fox affiliate in Boston was shooting on the street nearby and realized that an entertaining confrontation might ensue. So he started rolling as I strode over to greet Moore, who looked like somebody had just upchucked on his sneakers.

"You're running, Moore," I vamped to the camera. "You're not man enough to face me."

Moore is no fool about publicity and knew this was lead-story material for every Fox news program in the country. So he agreed almost at once to come on **The Factor** that night! It was great.

But, unfortunately, the interview wasn't great, at least not for me. Moore didn't debate, he filibustered. He repeated the same anti–Iraq war mantra over and over: "Would you send your son to Fallujah?" It was boring.

Dissenting from the Iraq war was not the problem. Millions, perhaps most, Americans have come to believe that the Iraq fight might not have been worth it. But on this occasion, I had a ton of questions about how Moore had handled his 9/11 film, and he simply didn't want to have a conversation. He wanted to vent against Bush. For me it was headache-inducing, although many viewers wrote saying they loved the shoot-out.

As I stated, I truly believe Michael Moore is no longer a factor (again, my apologies) in the culture war. Unwittingly, he has staked out Ralph Nader–like territory. As it stands now, he is not powerful enough to make a difference in American culture, not rational and persuasive enough to change minds. He'll talk his trash, make his money, and keep the baseball cap business in the black. But he's become a sideshow to the main event. George Soros wouldn't touch him.

Susan Sarandon: The actress and her common-law husband, Tim Robbins, epitomize the secular-progressive showbiz crowd. They are always on the S-P side, always touting the anti-traditionalist vision. But I have some respect for Ms. Sarandon, because she does put her money where her mouth is: She donates major dollars to help the poor.

As I explain in more detail in my book **The No Spin Zone**, the one appearance on **The Factor** by this fine actress came in the wake of a police shooting in New York City. An unarmed African immigrant, Amadou Diallo, was slain after some cops who were hunting for a rapist panicked after the lead officer fell down while attempting to question Mr. Diallo in a darkened hallway. This was an awful situation, but after all the evidence was presented, a twelve-person jury, including four African Americans, acquitted the police officers of any wrongdoing.

Now, it is Ms. Sarandon's view of America that minorities consistently have their rights violated by a system that is overly suspicious of them and callous in regard to their needs. She believes the United States is not "nurturing" the poor and disadvantaged; by this reasoning, high ghetto crime rates are basically society's fault. This is classic S-P thinking, of course, straight down the party line.

Remember, the Yoda of the S-P movement, George Lakoff, lists the lack of "broad prosperity" among the nation's poor as one of the major secular-progressive issues. By the term "broad

I once interviewed Susan Sarandon pre-**Factor** in the 1970s: Who has better hair?

prosperity," Lakoff means that the federal government should be obliged to provide poor Americans with just about everything middle-class Americans have. His word "provide" means giving money and material things to citizens. Thus, Lakoff's "broad prosperity" theory is really socialism. No other word for it. And S-P enthusiasts like Susan Sarandon buy into it.

Immediately after the Diallo shooting (that is, before any facts were established), Ms. Sarandon and other committed S-P foot soldiers organized antipolice rallies. That rankled me. I believe in giving the police the benefit of the doubt; in addition to the grandfather I mentioned earlier, I have friends who are cops. I know firsthand that most American law-enforcement officials are good people doing a tough job for relatively low pay. Most traditionalists, including me, give the cops the presumption of innocence. Susan Sarandon does not.

Surprisingly, on September 25, 2000, Ms. Sarandon agreed to come on **The Factor** to discuss the Diallo case. It was her first and last appearance. White-hot angry that the young man had been killed, she chalked the tragedy up to institutional racism and unabashedly despised my opposing point of view.

For example, when I pointed out that aggressive police work had caused a historic drop in black crime rates, especially in the inner city, she huffed and snapped back: "At what cost?"

Actually, the cost-benefit ratio is pretty obvious, if you take into account the drastic drop in the murder rate in many poor neighborhoods across the country. But we are obviously not talking rationality here. I mean, what I don't get about Susan Sarandon and her fellow S-P travelers is the constant anger. I actually found her opinions on the Diallo matter interesting, if wrongheaded. I wasn't upset that she disagreed with me—that's what I want on **The Factor.**

But she detested all of my rebuttals. After the interview in the greenroom (where **Factor** guests wait before going on the show), she blurted out: "What's **his** problem?"

I think it's safe to say that I will not be vacationing in the south of France with Susan and Tim anytime soon. It is a fact of life in the culture war that the S-P side is usually furious with the traditional opposition. And that fury hurts the S-P forces, as it clouds judgment and thinking. You lose the debate if you get mad without cause.

However, it is true that honest anger, when properly aimed at a legitimate target, can be a useful tool in the culture war. For example, the last time I appeared on Jon Stewart's program he asked me why I was (in his opinion) "constantly teed off." I replied that I have to deal with a massive amount of social injustice and chicanery on a daily basis and it takes a healthy amount of agita to deal with it all efficiently and effectively. Trying to right wrongs in this country will wear you down, but anger can keep you going when everybody else is exhausted. So, it's a tough situation for the traditional culture warrior: You need to keep the fires of indignation lighted but avoid the backdrafts.

I do understand—and it is absolutely true, by the way—that some traditionalists are captive to the same degree of irrational anger that many in the S-P crew are; you can hear that traditional rage daily on talk radio. But, for the most part, if you compare the S-P Web sites with the traditional ones, there is no doubt: S-P anger is far more intense and personal. Check it out, at the risk of your own mental well-being.

Alec Baldwin: And while we're on the subject of angry S-P guys, Mr. Baldwin stands front and center. Once again, the actor is primarily interested in politics, but there is always that progressive crossover: because he is a liberal Democrat, the S-P forces support his philosophy.

Like Susan Sarandon, Alec Baldwin is a first-rate actor who can convincingly bring to life a variety of characters. Check out his performance in **Glengarry Glen Ross.** It's brilliant. Yet Baldwin has not achieved the leading-man fame that was once predicted for him, and some believe his strident politics (calling Dick Cheney a madman, generally overreacting to conservative thought) have damaged him in the marketplace because some right-leaning Americans abhor his politics.

And it might be true. Alec Baldwin is a wounded S-P warrior, and I believe he knows it. After years of my trying to get an interview with him, Baldwin finally entered the No Spin Zone on August 9, 2004.

O'Reilly: "You haven't been as outspoken the past three years as you were before. Is there a reason for that?"

Baldwin: "Most Americans are choosing to get their predigested news information and opinion from folks like you and other commentators on this network [Fox Newschannel] and on other cable networks, and so forth, less so than on the networks. And I realized that the celebrity-activist thing was kind of a waste of time."

O'Reilly: "I've followed your career closely and I think your past activism hurt your career. Would I be wrong?"

Baldwin: "I would imagine that there are people who wouldn't hire me because they'd rather . . . Let's put it this way—the most successful people in my business are people that you know nothing about [politically]."

O'Reilly: "Tom Cruise?"

Baldwin: "You know nothing about them."

Ironically, Alec Baldwin and I were raised within miles of each other on Long Island. We are both Irish and our families were working class. So how could he and I "evolve" into such different culture warriors? I put that question to him.

"I would prefer to say I developed into one type of traditionalist," he said, "and you developed into another type of traditionalist."

"Would you rather I call you a progressive?" I shot back.

"I think the only word that can describe me is **Democrat.** I mean, I'm an outright partisan Democrat."

Okay, fine. But you don't feel the political burn the way Baldwin does just by being a member of a political party. No, he's an ardent S-P player who gets emotional about the state of the Union.

Personally, I like Baldwin, and think he's a well-intentioned guy despite the over-the-top outbursts, which could be a sign of immaturity or frustration. Off his crusade, Baldwin is smart and funny and not a bad softball player. But sometimes his anger causes him to lose it on the battlefield. A lesson learned for all culture warriors.

Jimmy Breslin: Another Irish secular-progressive who has lost it entirely. Again, the anger got him. In his day, Jimmy Breslin was one of the finest newspaper columnists New York City has ever seen. Only Pete Hamill, another talented Irish rogue, rivaled him for street smarts, empathy for the underdog, and storytelling ability. But, over the years, Breslin has degenerated into a remorseless smear merchant, primarily interested in damaging those who do not share his secular-progressive view on life. Although he is not an important figure on the national scene, my interaction with him is instructive in regard to S-P media types.

I've run into Breslin a number of times over the years and had always found him to be entertaining. That is, until he began writing for **Newsday**, the newspaper of Long Island. That financially troubled operation, which has been steadily losing circulation for years, allows its columnists to consistently hit below the belt. Breslin embraced that tactic and wildly attacked perceived villains, most of them traditional thinkers. His anti-Catholic columns, for example, were off-the-chart hateful. Some observers believe the Tribune Company, which owns **Newsday**, forced him to retire in order to air out the newsroom.

It should come as no surprise, then, that Jimmy Breslin dislikes me, a traditional culture warrior, with a vengeance. Over the years, I ignored his personal attacks directed my way, but when he tried to damage my book **The O'Reilly Factor for Kids,** I decided to drop him a little note.

In that short missive, I wrote in part: "You have tried to hurt a project that could help many children. Hope you feel good about that."

Not surprisingly, I never heard back from Breslin, who usually avoids direct confrontation. He's more comfortable with "drive-by" guttersniping than with actual debate.

One footnote: Breslin also had a book out at the time **Factor for Kids** was released. It was a brutal assault on the Roman Catholic Church and those who are loyal to it. Perhaps God took notice. Breslin's book sold fewer than 10,000 copies, while **The O'Reilly Factor for Kids** has sold more than 500,000 and is still selling. Chalk one up for the traditionalists.

Nancy Pelosi: Although I've never met the congresswoman from San Francisco (and, of course, the House minority leader), I have encountered her persona frequently through the media, so I guess you could say we have a "virtual" rapport.

Watching her over the years, I have seen few elected politicians whose S-P fever is as high as

Ms. Pelosi's. I mean, this woman is on **fire** for the secular-progressive cause.

My most memorable Pelosi encounter was sparked by my criticism of a ballot measure that banned all military recruiting in the schools of San Francisco, including college campuses. In November 2005, San Francisco voters disrespected the U.S. military, currently fighting a vicious war on terror, by voting 60 percent to 40 percent to restrict recruiting. The vote was purely symbolic—in other words, a cheap shot—because if the city actually did ban military recruiting in the schools, it stood to lose federal funding. And with all the progressive programs the City by the Bay embraces, that would be Armageddon.

Anyway, on **The Radio Factor**, I did a riff that said okay, fine, if San Francisco didn't want the U.S. military around, they should form their own militia. I then painted a scenario that blew the lid off the left-wing smear Web sites that monitor **The Radio Factor** every day. My exact comments were these:

"And if al-Qaeda comes in and blows you up, we're not going to do anything about it. We're going to say, 'Look, every other place in America is off-limits to you except San Francisco. You want to blow up the Coit Tower, go ahead.' "

Well, you would have thought I suggested blowing up the Coit Tower! Wait a minute, isn't that what I did? Uh-oh.

Actually, this is standard talk-radio stuff, intentionally using hyperbole to make a point. In its initial reporting on the incident, even the far-left **San Francisco Chronicle** reasonably pointed that out. Surely, we all know that people listen to talk radio to be entertained as well as informed. Otherwise, why would any sane person listen? Come on! The vote in question clearly demonstrated that San Franciscans did not want the military around, so I took that fact to an absurd level. (Some of you overstudious types may remember the debating technique called **reductio ad absurdum.**) The point I was **trying** to make was that in this very intense time for our national security, we all owe allegiance to the military whether we support the way the terror war is being fought or not. My delivery was purposely over-the-top, and my cohost, E. D. Hill, wryly chastised me during the entire riff. No rational person could have taken the al-Qaeda part of the monologue seriously.

Except one.

Quick as a cat with a train bearing down on it, Nancy Pelosi leaped into the fray and cried out her outrage:

> Bill O'Reilly's comments about San Francisco are simply outside the circle of civilized discussion. There is no place in responsible journalism **to call for a terrorist attack** [boldface mine] against any American city, let alone the beautiful and dynamic city of San Francisco, which has contributed so much to America's military, civic, and cultural history. Mr. O'Reilly's comments are not a joke; they are not acceptable. He should apologize.

Congresswoman Pelosi then summed up with a threat: "And Fox goes ahead on this at its own peril."

Yikes! And that wasn't the end of the matter. After Pelosi's comments, the San Francisco Board of Supervisors approved a resolution urging Fox News to fire me. I'm not kidding. On the public's dime, the loopy supervisors passed resolution number 818-5, which stated in part: "Whereas, Mr. O'Reilly's remarks constitute a flagrant disregard for the safety and welfare of San Franciscans and inciting acts of terrorism; now, therefore be it RESOLVED, that the Board of Supervisors hereby urges Fox News Corporation and Westwood One to terminate the employment of news show host Bill O'Reilly for speech condoning acts of terrorism."

Maybe I shouldn't buy a condo in the Haight after all.

Of course, we immediately invited Nancy Pelosi on **The Factor** to hash things out—predictably she declined, as did Mayor Gavin Newsome, who signed the nutty resolution.

Much to my dismay because the publicity was great, the whole thing blew over in two days, even though the **Chronicle** tried to fan the flames. Our radio affiliate in San Francisco, KNEW, played my monologue a number of times so everybody could hear it, and their hosts had a great time mocking City Hall.

But over on the dark side, the S-P army thought they had something big, and some smear Web sites even tried to organize a sponsor boycott of **The Radio Factor.** Oh, the outrage!

In the end, though, fanaticism and hypocrisy once again did in the S-Ps. Anyone who has ever listened to the secular-progressive propaganda mill Air America knows that I am a piker when it comes to on-air "satire." Those AA people make me look about as dangerous as Paula Abdul.

As for Nancy Pelosi, what you see is what the secular-progressive movement gets. She is a top S-P standard-bearer who lives in a virtual Land of Oz. And to her I have only one thing to say: You better knock it off, lady, or I'll throw water on you and take your shoes.

Of course, I've had many more S-P close encounters, but to tell you the truth, writing about them exhausts me. There is no reasoning with most of these people, no way to debate them with energy and then, afterward, have a beer with them. They are committed, determined, and live in a permanent "no traditionalist zone." You will not persuade, convince, or mollify them. If you are on the traditional side, the S-Ps will reject you and perhaps try to inflict pain upon your person. Of that there is no question.

Finally, if you don't believe what I've just told you, just watch what happens after this book hits the marketplace. First, the advance S-P guard in the press will deny a culture war exists (even as I write, a columnist in the showbiz newspaper **Variety** has done just that), the same tactic they used in the Christmas controversy.

"O'Reilly is making the whole thing up to sell books," they'll write. "There's no culture war in this country. It's a cynical fabrication designed to sell books"—that will replace "designed to get ratings" from the 9/11 and Christmas controversies.

The denial strategy will be for public consumption. But behind the scenes, the S-P power brokers will be seething, and I guarantee they will command their forces to attack me in every way possible. As in the past, personal smears will rule the day and I will be defamed from all secular directions. Sadly, I'm used to that kind of vitriol. The flaming arrows in the S-P war plan keep coming; the more effective a traditionalist is, the more arrows will be launched into the air. In a weird way, I guess I should be flattered. But it does get very old.

No question, the S-P leadership, as well as their sympathizers in the media, will not at all like the exposition you are reading. Laying bare the secular-progressive agenda and their strategy of imposing it on America leaves the S-Ps exposed. That, of course, will anger them. The smear campaign will likely begin on the Net, quickly spread to left-wing newspaper columnists, and then go on to the Fox-hating MSNBC network. Of course, there will be a counterattack by me and other traditional forces, because hatred must be answered with resolve and facts. It's going to be nasty. Just wait and see.

Some things are inevitable, and at this point in the culture war, trying to **damage** the opposition, rather than discredit its ideas with fact-based logical argument, has become the primary game plan of the S-P movement. To be fair, some traditional forces use smear tactics as well, but again, not nearly on the level that the S-Ps use them.

And so we march on. This book will intensify the fight and, I hope, might also convince some Americans not fully engaged in the culture war to step up and support the good guys: us.

If that happens, the S-Ps are doomed, because the vast majority of Americans, according to the polls, believe the United States is a good country and that Judeo-Christian values continue to provide a foundation for justice and prosperity. Most Americans, therefore, don't want a drastic restructuring of the country and are firmly in the traditional camp. But, I'll submit, many potential culture warriors on the traditional side don't have a clue as to what is going on. They are a great untapped resource.

The question then becomes: Why are so many traditionalists disengaged? On paper, it doesn't make much sense.

Consider that, overwhelmingly, Americans oppose gay marriage, partial-birth abortion, legalized drugs, the banishment of spirituality in the public square, and most other core S-P issues. Did you know that 87 percent of counties in the United States do not have one physician who will perform an abortion? Why is that? Could it be that most doctors and Americans in general are uncomfortable with this anti-life procedure?

Doing the math once again, we see that it all adds up to a decidedly traditional country, does it not? At this point, the prevailing wisdom among both the Republican and Democratic Party operatives is that 15 percent of Americans are hard-core liberal, 35 percent conservative, and the rest moderate or apolitical. Those numbers come from internal polling done by both parties.

But you'd never know that liberalism is embraced by so few by listening to the media, would you? To many who consider themselves the elite in the United States, S-P doctrine is attractive and comforting. No God to worry about, a "nurturing posture" toward the poor, and an "enlightened" philosophy of government and, indeed, of life. The S-P view of the world really takes the edge off the "consumer guilt" of some who are living large in the wealthy precincts. Yeah, we may be greed heads, but we're enlightened greed heads, they might admit (under hypnosis).

But most Americans do not have "consumer guilt" because they live normal, economical lives. Yet despite being outnumbered, the S-Ps, mostly hard-core liberals, are still very active on the battlefield and, in some states, traditional forces are suffering. How can that be happening, with the numbers skewed so strongly toward the traditional? The next pages will provide the answer.

PART 3

The Struggle for the Soul of America

Twelve

Who Will Win the Culture War?

> The world is filled with concern but also with hypocrisy. Hypocrisy on the part of people who see no evil and speak no evil to avoid becoming involved.
>
> —MARCELLO PERA

So which side are you on in the culture war? Or are you sitting things out? If you truly love your country, these are key questions, because if the secular-progressive vision becomes reality, your love interest will mutate right before your eyes. Think it over. This culture war deal might just be worth your time and attention.

Right now, it is the conservative Christian groups that are most engaged on the traditional side, and their interest stems primarily from theology. The secular-progressives despise groups like Focus on the Family and The Christian Coalition because their members tend to judge the S-Ps along moral lines and, generally, condemn their behavior and aspirations. There is nothing that angers the S-P forces more than to be told they do **not** hold the high moral ground.

But I don't believe this culture war will be won in the religious arena. Even though the Christian groups are effective in getting their traditional message out, they are outgunned. In order to stop the S-P movement cold, nonreligious Americans have to be persuaded that traditionalism is in their best interest. The most powerful nonreligious argument against the S-P agenda is that it is simply better public policy for the United States to stay close to the vision of the Founders, which includes independence from big government, hard work, personal responsibility, and looking out for your neighbor.

Remember, the S-Ps want a **huge** government apparatus to dispense their notion of "economic justice." They envision an enormous centralized force in Washington that would **nurture** its citizens from cradle to grave (at the expense of others, of course). This utopian dream is impossible, especially in a land of 300 million people, but the S-Ps will never believe that. If they gain power, your assets will become their assets. On the foreign-policy front, our government will become a cog in a "one world" consolidation of power ruled by global consensus—

a kind of United Nations on steroids. Add to that the permissive social environment the S-Ps so desperately espouse and, presto, the United States as we've known it for 230 years will disappear.

Yes, I may have overstated things a bit in the above paragraph, but not by much. The truth is that there are varying levels of fanaticism in the S-P ranks. As with every movement, there are both militants and moderates in the S-P army, but they all have one thing in common: They want a far different America from the one in which we are living today. Okay, I'll say it once again: The secular-progressive dream is not an impossible one for them to achieve—largely because so many traditional Americans are ignoring the escalating culture war. An unfortunate example of this is the Roman Catholic Church in America, which has largely been missing in action as far as the culture war is concerned. As a Catholic, I'm perplexed and disappointed by this. Right now, American Protestants are really doing most of the heavy lifting on the traditional side. Jewish Americans are divided; in fact, some of the most fanatical secular-progressives are Jewish (are you listening, Barbra?). But the nation's more than 67 million Catholics have certainly not been encouraged by their leadership to enter the fray.

With the exception of Archbishop Michael Sheehan of Santa Fe, New Mexico, I know of no high-ranking Catholic cleric in America who consistently speaks out against the secular-progressive agenda. Most of the official Catholic energy is devoted to the pro-life movement. Of course, S-Ps adamantly support unfettered abortion. Their agenda includes legal partial-birth abortion, no parental notification when minors abort, and no spousal notification, either. All of this comes under the banner of a woman's "reproductive rights." As I mentioned earlier, destroying a soon-to-be-born baby by extracting its head from the mother's womb and putting a piece of steel through the base of the baby's skull (that's the partial-birth abortion procedure) doesn't sound very "nurturing" to me, but the S-P forces have no problem with it.

Anyway, the Catholic hierarchy does stand up on the abortion issue; however, when faced with other culture war issues, they recede back into the sacristies. But why? Surely, the Church understands what has happened in Europe, where secular culture has replaced the traditional religious landscape. Countries like Spain, France, and Italy, once devoutly Catholic, have now moved away from organized religion and are increasingly embracing secular culture. The free fall of tradition is most noticeable in Northern Europe, where the percentage of people attending weekly church services is down to the single digits in places like Holland and Scandinavia. Even in Italy, the historic seat of the Catholic Church, attendance at mass has plummeted as the secular-progressive culture has swept away traditional beliefs.

To replace this loss of spirituality, millions of Europeans have embraced the secular concept of "relativism." According to this way of thinking, there is no absolute truth, no certain right and wrong. Everything is "relative." What is wrong in my eyes might not be wrong in your eyes. By this logic, even heinous acts can be explained, so they should not—in fact, they cannot—be condemned. In other words, no definite judgments about behavior should be made because there are always extenuating circumstances to justify not taking a stand.

The wide acceptance of relativism has rendered Europe weak, confused, and chaotic. Socialist or quasi-socialist governments now provide the necessities of life to their citizens, allowing many Europeans to live entirely within themselves. When that happens to a person, it is hard to rally him or her to a greater cause. Thus, nothing is worth fighting for outside of one's immediate well-being. The only creed is a belief in personal gratification.

The president of the Italian Senate, Marcello Pera, has recognized the danger especially in how it pertains to fighting the international war on terror, which much of Europe refuses to do. In the book **Without Roots,** Pera writes:

> Crisis is an overused word these days, but in the present circumstances of Europe it is, unfortunately, appropriate . . . relativism has wreaked havoc, and it continues to act as a mirror and an echo chamber for the dark mood that has fallen over the West. It has paralyzed the West, when it is already disoriented and at a standstill, rendered it defenseless when it is already acquiescent, and confused it when it is already reluctant to rise to the challenge.
>
> How can we speak of, and defend, "universal human rights" in a cultural climate in which the very idea of "truth" is under sustained assault?

The answer to Pera's question is that you cannot defend the human rights of others if you believe the only thing worth fighting for is yourself. Remember this: Much of Europe was perfectly willing to do business with Saddam

Hussein and allow him to murder at will, even after he invaded Kuwait in 1990. These days, most of the European press expresses far more outrage over President Bush than they ever did about Saddam, or even Osama bin Laden. The truth is that much of Europe will not confront Islamo-fascism and will not support the United States in the war on terror because that would mean putting their own butts on the line. Yes, I know some NATO countries have provided troops in Afghanistan, and that Great Britain, a blessed exception to the European rule, is America's most reliable ally. But when it comes to crunch time against a nuclear-minded Iran, or a terrorist-supporting Syria, or another 9/11-type attack here or abroad, do you really expect to see most Europeans step up?

I don't.

Far more than most institutions, the Catholic Church has been able to see and experience firsthand the rise of secular-progressive thought and the decline of European power and influence. Yet in the United States, which thus far has rejected the relativist philosophy of the secular-progressives, the Church is a nonfactor in the culture war. Every Sunday at mass, I pray that will change.

It is frustrating to me to sit in the church pew and listen to the priest explain St. Paul's letters to the Corinthians for the 876th time. What I want to know is how St. Paul, a Roman warrior and pagan activist before conversion, would see today's culture war. If Jesus were alive on earth right now, would he be a traditionalist? If so, why? Once in a while, a priest will discuss a social issue from his pulpit, but that's rare.

What traditional Americans need desperately is leadership along with a clarification of which traditional values are worth fighting for and why. But don't expect that leadership to come from Washington or your state capital. Like the American Catholic bishops, most politicians fear the culture war. It is too emotional and controversial. Better to lock themselves into a party and ideology than to confront day-to-day issues that directly affect Americans. That would be too messy. And every elected official knows that the secular press would come after them with a vengeance if they enlisted on the side of traditionalists in the culture war.

Because of that prevailing wisdom, conservatives like President Bush, and even moderate liberals like President Clinton, avoid the culture war almost entirely. And the lesser lights on Capitol Hill follow that lead. No culture war for them.

One exception to that rule is Howard Dean. As much as I dislike what the governor stands for, he is an S-P warrior front and center. No question about that. In fact, Congresswoman Pelosi and Dean are the two most engaged American politicians in the culture war today. Sadly, they are on the wrong side.

One of the political issues that have crossed party lines and trotted onto the culture war battlefield is the gay rights debate. According to a Pew Research Center poll taken in the spring of 2006, 50 percent of Americans feel that homosexual behavior is morally wrong, just 12 percent feel it is morally acceptable, and 33 percent do not see it as a moral issue at all. But in this area, some traditionalists have chosen to make a stand. And that may be a mistake.

Recently, Catholic Charities got out of the adoption business in Massachusetts after that S-P state demanded that the Catholic organization actively help gays adopt children, a practice the Church opposes. Now, I happen to favor allowing children consigned to foster care to live in a gay home when no other alternative is available. There is no question that children thrive in a loving environment, and there is no question that having a mother and a father is what Nature intended. But we live in the real world of the twenty-first century. If it's between a kid bouncing around a chaotic, sometimes dangerous child-care system and being placed in a stable home with honest people who very much want the abandoned child, I am in favor of the latter. And I'm not basing my opinion on emotion. A variety of scientific studies have shown that kids raised by gay parents usually turn out the same way children in traditional homes do. Remember, the traditional warrior fights with facts.

But I will listen to the other point of view and am very interested in hearing exactly why the Catholic Church disagrees with me on this issue. But I have heard little. No solid reasoning was put forth by Catholic Charities other than upholding the Church's position that homosexual conduct is wrong.

A long time ago, I decided to leave the judgments about sin to the Deity. I believe that falls under His or Her job description. Since every human being is a sinner, we should all concentrate on healing ourselves. Whatever Larry and Lenny and Penny and Connie are doing is none of my business. By the way, privacy is a traditional value.

But I do understand that gay marriage has an impact on straight marriage, which of course is a bedrock traditional institution. And there is a good reason why American society is built around the traditional heterosexual home. As a societal stabilizer, traditional marriage deserves a special place in our national life. Homosexuality is an alternative situation. There are many other alternative situations, such as polygamy, triads, and whatever Paris Hilton comes up with next. Again, morally, the Deity can sort this out. But the United States, in my opinion, is under no obligation to change the traditional definition of marriage so everybody can feel good about themselves.

Now, I realize I am not telling you something new. According to every poll and actual votes on referendums, as I've noted before, Americans overwhelmingly support the special status heterosexual marriage has in the United States. In my mind, there is no compelling reason to alter that status, especially if the states approve legal partnerships so that citizens are not denied things like hospital visitations, participation in end-of-life decision making, and insurance coverage.

By the way, traditional warriors do not base their philosophy on bigotry, as many S-P propaganda merchants charge. We look at what is best for the country. We can see the decency in respecting all legal partnerships Americans choose for themselves. But altering the traditional fabric of society is not necessary in order to do that.

Unfortunately, the Catholic Church, like many other religious organizations, provides none of the above analysis. Its approach to this issue is all based around "sin." That approach plays directly into the hands of the secular-progressives, who loudly wail that religious intrusion into society is un-Constitutional and demonize religious leaders who dare to speak out. Maybe that is why most American Catholic leaders remain silent in the face of the culture war. Like the politicians, they don't want to become targets. The priest-pedophilia scandal proved that Catholic leadership was weak. The lack of engagement in the culture war is another demonstration of that.

To be fair (a hallmark of the traditional warrior), it is certainly true that if a religious person does wander onto the cultural battlefield, he or she better have a strong stomach, because he or she has a good chance of being demonized.

Stanley Kurtz, contributing editor for **National Review Online**, sums it up this way:

> The fact of the matter is that the Left's [S-Ps'] rhetorical attacks on conservative Christians [traditionalists] have long been more extreme, more widely disseminated, and more politically effective than whatever the Christians have been hurling back. And now that their long ostracism by the media has finally forced conservative Christians to

demand redress, the Left has abandoned all rhetorical restraint.

Kurtz points to a number of examples. On April 24, 2005, the S-P fanatic Frank Rich, writing in the **New York Times,** compared conservative Christians to George Wallace, segregationists, and lynch mobs.

In a similar vein, Christopher Hedges, a former **New York Times** writer, produced an article in **Harper's** magazine called "Feeling the Hate with the National Religious Broadcasters." Hedges patched together a series of vitriolic statements by Pat Robertson and other religious broadcast pundits to selectively paint the picture that the religious right is nuts. This is standard issue for S-P magazine writers: dig up kooky quotes and print them without context. Any writer can do that to any subject. It's simple but off-the-chart dishonest.

That is not to say there have not been nutty statements made by the traditional side; there clearly have been. But think about this: Every time Jerry Falwell or Pat Robertson or anybody on the right goes over the line, it is played big in the mainstream media. But if an S-P player uses loony rhetoric, like calling all Americans who oppose gay marriage bigots, well, many in the American media have no problem with that. So, to use a cliché, the deck is stacked.

That being said, the traditional warrior would be well advised to avoid personal attacks and over-the-top rhetoric. Sure, that kind of thing makes the savage running the "Savage Nation" on the radio millions, but irresponsible bomb-throwing doesn't further the traditional cause. The traditionalist warrior should expect to be slimed and defamed and mocked, and should fight back with facts and rational argument. That takes courage and self-restraint. Believe me, I often want to deck those who attack me. That's a natural reaction. But the effective warrior knows the battle will not be won in the mud or by losing control.

As I mentioned in the beginning of this book, there is a difference between challenging people on their portrayal of the issues and attacking them by using defamation, rumormongering and name-calling. These are **ad hominem** ("to the man" in Latin) attacks. As a traditionalist who wants to win the fight, I try to avoid the personal stuff.

Sometimes I make a mistake, but I **know** it's a mistake. Win the debate on the issues; let the smear merchants do the guttersniping.

So you can see that Americans who choose to fight in the culture war will not have an easy time of it. That, of course, is why so many potential warriors remain on the sidelines. In light of that situation, here's one more suggestion to Americans of faith and for other traditionalists, too: There are thousands of good clergypeople in the United States who are trying to fight the good fight in the culture war. These people need your encouragement. The Christmas controversy proved that traditional causes can triumph if faith-based organizations mobilize. The companies and groups that sought to diminish displays of the Christmas season were crushed by the opposition. That's how you win the culture war: Speak up clearly and often, then get ready to absorb the slings and flaming arrows. Summon up your courage and confront situations you believe are damaging to your country.

By the very nature of its philosophy, traditionalism is on the defensive. We are defending the country we have, while the S-Ps are working for drastic change that would produce a country they want. In many situations this is a drawback, as it is easier to fight battles when you are charging. For example, a person who seems to oppose everything will not be the most popular person around the campfire. But someone who wants to take action to make things "better" . . . well, that's the person who is admired, right?

The S-P brain trust knows this and has developed a crafty strategy for marginalizing traditionalist forces in the court of public opinion. The presentation is almost masterly, but as with all S-P campaigns, it does have a crippling weakness. Read on.

Thirteen

As American as Apple Pie?

The truth, the whole truth, and nothing but the truth. So help me, nothing.

—THE S-P OATH (REFERENCE TO DEITY DELETED BY THE SUPREME COURT IN THE YEAR OF OUR NOTHING 2010)

Read the following on page 110 of George Lakoff's **Elephant** book and weep:

> Progressive thought is **as American as apple pie** [italics mine]. Progressives want political equality, good public schools, healthy children, care for the aged, police protection, family farms, air you can breathe, water you can drink, fish in our streams, forests you can hike in, songbirds and frogs, livable cities, ethical businesses, journalists who tell the truth, music and dance, poetry and art, and jobs that pay a living wage to everyone who works.

Wow! Where do I sign up? That progressive vision is amazing, and what kind of a Visigoth barbarian would oppose it? I mean, who doesn't want songbirds? What kind of a brutish cad would deny frogs to children? Get me George Soros on the phone immediately; I've got to apologize!

Wait a minute, not so fast, overly impressionable culture warrior. After all, we're not taking a political science class at Yale here. This book is real life, no spin, the true picture of what is actually happening in America. Lakoff is a propaganda genius; I'll give him his due. But let's examine his Edenic "vision" in a methodical, fact-based way.

We'll begin with one of the most successful S-P tactics: If you oppose their agenda, you are a bad person. A pro-life American is "anti–woman's rights." Against gay marriage? Well, you're designated as homophobic and terminally bigoted. Support an aggressive strategy to fight terrorism? You're labeled a warmonger; worse yet, if you take that stand but didn't yourself serve in the military, you are smeared as a "chicken hawk." Nice S-P strategy, right?

But George Lakoff understands that the primary culture war battle in America is to win "hearts and minds." He has no problem with the "defame and destroy" wing of the S-P movement, but his energies are more focused on the positive. Thus his "apple pie" list of S-P virtues.

So let's start our analysis with "political equality." How can we oppose **that**? Talk about a traditional value! All Americans should have the right to vote and the right to speak their mind about politics without fear of harm. I believe that is guaranteed by the Constitution and there are legal remedies if violations of political equality occur. Am I wrong? So what is Comrade Lakoff talking about?

To unmask the S-P agenda in this case, we go to the great state of Georgia, where the legislature recently passed a law requiring a voter to produce a valid ID before casting his or her ballot. The measure was aimed at stopping voter fraud—that is, people voting more than once—as well as voting by illegal aliens ("economic refugees" in S-P–speak). Everybody I know thought the Georgia law was reasonable.

But guess who has opposed that ID law? Hello again, ACLU, we missed you in the last few pages. The S-P vanguard is challenging the legislation in court by arguing that it puts an "undue burden" on the poor. The ACLU asserts that some poor folks don't have official identification papers and, even though Georgia will provide IDs free of charge, it is not fair to demand that a citizen get a valid ID. Does this make any sense to you?

The real reason the S-Ps don't want IDs at polling stations is that they would, indeed, eliminate the illegal alien vote, which is often cast for liberal, progressive candidates. Also, IDs would make it more difficult for people to be bused to polls out of their districts. This old-style machine-politics trick, unfortunately, happens quite often on Election Day. If I could get George Lakoff on **The Factor,** I'd ask him why his pals at the ACLU are so opposed to the government knowing exactly who is voting. After all, Lakoff says he wants "political equality," and that's what one vote per each legal American citizen achieves, does it not?

Let's march ahead to the concept of "good" public schools. How could anyone oppose those? All Americans want children to learn in the best way possible. But the S-P definition of a "good" public school may not be the same as yours and mine.

The "No Child Left Behind Act" poured billions of dollars into America's schools but, at the same time, instituted strict achievement standards—testing—to measure whether or not the school was succeeding in educating the kids. In other words, there is academic accountability to go along with the highest educational spending in America's history.

But progressives oppose standardized tests. They also don't want teacher evaluations based upon the academic proficiency of the students they teach. Furthermore, as mentioned, the S-Ps oppose vouchers to help poor children attend private schools when their public schools are deficient, and they want students promoted even when they fail in their subjects.

So doing even more of the math, this book does demand academic proficiency; what Lakoff and other progressive thinkers consider "good public schools" are places where teachers "nurture" rather than challenge children in the classroom. S-P schools would embrace the concept of "social promotion," where kids move along from grade to grade even if they can't read or do basic arithmetic. The S-P educational view features a system where each child is evaluated academically based on his or her "potential," not his or her actual achievement.

As a former teacher, I can tell you that the concept of "nurturing" is very nice, but it isn't going to get the kid into Princeton or even into many state colleges. Most children are lazy and undisciplined—that is a given—and must be **taught** to perform in a disciplined manner and develop a thinking process and marketable skills. Discipline and confidence are the key attributes for academic success and, indeed, success in life. We live in a very competitive society, and all the "nurturing" in the world is not going to get somebody a good job or help the young person succeed in it. Somebody tell Lakoff.

Okay, by cutting through the S-P bull, you can already see that Lakoff's "apple pie" list is not what it seems to be. So now on to the next item: "healthy children." Again, who doesn't want that? How can that worthy goal be distorted? Ahem.

The S-P vision "healthy children" mantra goes way beyond supplying the kid with carrots and apples. In the secular-progressive world, the "healthy" child is one who enters the school system as early as possible, is shepherded through childhood by public school nannies, and indoctrinated with progressive values at a very early age.

Rob Reiner, the actor-director, is the secular-progressive poster boy for this particular philosophy. Until he resigned in the winter of 2005, Reiner headed up the early-school programs in California. The organization he was a part of is called the California Children and Families Commission. To be fair, the commission does achieve much good, especially for little kids living in chaotic homes who are able to get preschooling free of charge. But Reiner ran into trouble by politicizing the program and running up huge expenses implementing it (including TV ads that promoted his progressive vision). So he had to quit, although expanded preschool ed is here to stay. And there is no question that the S-Ps are banking on progressive values being instilled into young minds during these early-school programs. That is the hidden agenda.

Our pal Professor Lakoff next cites "care for aged." Here he wants the government to pay all the bills for elderly Americans who have limited means. If you oppose that, of course, you are a monster. Universal support of the elderly is a major platform for the advocates of the entitlement society, and lots of senior citizens vote, do they not? So the S-Ps are trying to get on the fast track by targeting the very young and the very old.

Fifth is police protection. If you don't belong to the Crips, the Bloods, or al-Qaeda, you're surely down (a "hood" expression) with wanting that. However, progressive policing is far different from traditional policing. As Walter Cronkite and Randy Cohen have aptly demonstrated in previous pages, the S-P theorists of justice define crime quite differently from the way traditionalists do. Remember the "restorative justice" philosophy we talked about? That is what the S-Ps want the police to buy into. The rights and well-being of the criminal must be considered by society if "true" justice is to be achieved.

On the "family farms" issue, I think Lakoff and I might have finally found common soil. I like family farms, too. But I don't want to pay for them, just as I don't want to pay for somebody to run a clothing store. Nothing personal; it's just that capitalism requires competition and independent initiative. Although he didn't say it, I believe Lakoff would probably bill me for some agricultural project. As farmer McDonald might say: E-I-E-I ouch.

The next helpings of "apple pie" slices are environmental. Lakoff and the S-Ps want clean air, water, forests, and mountains. And, yes, they really want lots of frogs and songbirds.

Well, so do I. So there.

The Lakoff list continues with livable cities and ethical businesses. Those are good things. I hope George can provide them without kneecapping the taxpayer. But, somehow, I suspect massive taxation would be attached to any plan involving cities that are "livable," as opposed to cities that are full of the walking dead (for S-Ps, those are conservatives).

As for ethical businesses, I believe George would like a massive government to directly oversee them. Perhaps Fidel Castro could consult on this project.

Now we come to "journalists who tell the truth." Uh-oh. This could be bad news for me, since Lakoff is on record as condemning everything that has ever happened on the Fox Newschannel. Something tells me ol' George does not believe I am an honest correspondent. How desperately misguided the professor is.

But if George Lakoff could ever force American journalists to tell the truth, I might even send a donation to the ACLU. That is, if he actually starts where the problem truly lies, maybe with the nutty radical-left S-P bastion Air America. Good luck, George, and when you're through with them, check out NPR.

The Lakoff list winds down with "music and dance, poetry and art." As before, it's clear he wants you and me to pay for that wonderful vision in which we'd all be doing the tango and painting socially commendable murals. I wonder what ol' George thought of that art exhibition in the New York City–financed Brooklyn Museum that featured the Virgin Mary covered with dung? His ACLU buddies had no problem with it. Freedom of expression, you know. And I helped finance that sacrilege with my tax dollars.

As for poetry, well, how about this next incident? While serving as the poet laureate of New Jersey, Amiri Baraka wrote a verse blaming the Jews for the attack on 9/11. Taxpayers provided Baraka's hateful forum. Why? Why do regular folks have to pick up the tab for nutty "artists"? There's plenty of room for artistic expression in the private sector, is there not? What say you, George Lakoff?

Finally, for the last piece of Lakoff's apple pie, we are served with "jobs that pay a living wage to everyone who works." Pardon me, but isn't this right out of the Mao playbook? Just who determines what that wage should be? Not the actual employer, not on your life. Some government official would decide what Wal-Mart should pay its stock people, and the ruling S-P class would make the calls on "income inequality." This is called "socialism." Right, George?

So there you have it. In the end, that once-sweet apple pie list of great things for America might have a bit of a sour downside if you really analyze what's going on. The menu looks appetizing; the actual meal is quite something else. It is my job as a media culture warrior to sift through the ingredients. That is why you're reading this book.

For all the songbirds and frogs and healthy kids and happy seniors, there would be a huge central apparatus that would have to implement and monitor those things—an impersonal authority that would be extremely powerful and expensive. George Orwell figured that out long ago in his **Animal Farm,** and so did Aldous Huxley in **Brave New World,** two books that are required reading for the traditional warrior officer corps.

And, after finishing that reading assignment, you'll know for certain that the S-P vision of George Lakoff is, indeed, a brave new world.

Fourteen

Hating America

> Whenever any form of government becomes destructive . . . it is the right of the people to alter or abolish it.
>
> —HUEY NEWTON, FOUNDER OF THE BLACK PANTHER PARTY

Roger Ailes is the president of Fox News and a humorous guy. He has been known to attend cocktail parties in Manhattan, a bastion of secular-progressive thought, and when an S-P person sounds off about the dismal state of the United States, Ailes will sometimes loudly respond: "Why do you hate America?"

That's a room silencer if there ever was one.

There is nothing worse you can do to a devoted S-P acolyte than imply that he or she is unpatriotic. I mean, the actor Richard Dreyfuss recently did about twenty minutes on that in front of the National Press Club in Washington, D.C. He was appalled that some conservatives questioned his love of country: For the record, my name was mentioned in the diatribe.

But, of course, I never questioned Dreyfuss's patriotism or anything else about the man (except, perhaps, his agreeing to play a character named Duddy Kravitz).

In fact, Richard Dreyfuss is absolutely correct in asserting there is no place for personal, rhetorical attacks that charge lack of patriotism. It is flat-out wrong to question the loyalty of any American unless there is rock-solid proof that the person is trying to damage the country. In my opinion, Dreyfuss is doing nothing of the sort.

Remember, there are varying degrees of S-P behavior. Some secular-progressives, perhaps including the actor, are sincerely committed to improving the United States. They are generally reasonable folks who are simply misguided in their beliefs. Others, however, are fanatics who genuinely believe America is a wicked country that must be reformed in any way possible short of violence in the streets (there are very few S-P Huey Newtons). That is what the Soros crowd believes, and they are currently leading the secular-progressive movement.

So it does happen that members of the two opposing forces, secular-progressives and traditionalists, can similarly love and respect their country but also disagree as to how the country should be run. That situation can lead to lively debate and, sometimes, to an exchange of valid points. Sadly, however, those interactions are as rare as tax-cut proposals from the S-P side. Hatred is far more common on the culture war battlefield than détente.

A good example of a useful face-off between polar opposites was my interview with Norman Mailer in March 2006. One of America's great writers, Mailer doesn't hate America but does find it seriously flawed—as you know, a core secular-progressive tenet. But Mailer separates himself from the S-P garrison because he sees its weakness: selfishness and relativism. Remember, if you are a relativist there are no universal truths for you—no judgments about absolute rights or wrongs. Norman Mailer makes judgments all day long.

Along with his son, Mailer wrote **The Big Empty**, a book in which he expounded on life, liberty, and the pursuit of happiness. On **The Radio Factor**, I quizzed him about his essential beliefs and found him conflicted. Most S-Ps are not conflicted, they are dead certain they are right. But, at age

Norman Mailer, an S-P warrior who defines the issues at stake in the culture war in the clearest terms.

eighty-two, Mailer isn't quite so sure anymore that he has the answers.

The author frames the culture war argument in liberal-conservative terms, which is a mistake. As I've argued, the true culture battle is us against them: traditionalists versus secular-progressives. But old-school Mailer defines the war this way:

> A great war is going on here, larger even than we realize, between the liberals and the conservatives. The conservatives are saying, in effect, "You guys are trying to wreck existence by becoming too vain, too Godless." And liberals are replying, "Your obsession that God is judgmental looks to force all of humanity into rigid patterns that won't work any longer." The worst is that they are both right. It's a war between extremes, and they are both right.

But Mailer is wrong. Traditional Americans and conservative thinkers who **understand their country** do not put God at the head of public policy, nor do we point fingers at the opposition and label them "sinners." We label them "intellectually deficient." Traditionalists believe that secular-progressive policies will weaken America and lead to societal chaos. While we see no reason to banish God from the public square, we don't expect Him to be writing social policy on tablets and handing them to us in the Sinai.

Norman Mailer has come to the conclusion that the United States is in decline because traditional thinking and capitalism have uprooted true "democratic" principles. Mailer told me on the radio that he favors a huge central government that would "regulate" the profits of corporations and the incomes of Americans. He would like to see social engineering—that is, a society that is **forced** to be generous and fair. That vision would, of course, require a good amount of totalitarianism, a system Mailer abhors.

Finally, like many S-P warriors, Norman Mailer sees American power weakening and he's somewhat happy about it. He explains that on page 105 of **Empty:**

> It may be that we would do well to recognize (and this will be an odious remark to a

great many Americans) that the apex of our power has passed. We are now a very powerful nation in a world of three or four other very powerful nations. If we could make our peace with that, my guess is that terrorist acts against us might diminish. Because one aspect of present terrorism is the reaction to our arrogance.

Of course, the traditional culture warrior (T-Warrior) does not buy this. I believe that if the United States demonstrates the slightest weakness in the face of Islamo-fascism, we will be attacked more readily. I point to the appeasement of the fanatical Third Reich about seventy years ago to back up my opinion. There is no difference in attitude between the Nazis and the jihadists. Those who do not learn from history are condemned to repeat it.

But while I disagree with him, I concede that Norman Mailer clearly defines some very important issues in the intense culture war. The secular-progressive movement **wants** the United States to decline in power. It **wants** a new world order where global consensus would rule and the superpower model of our time would recede into obsolescence.

By contrast, the T-Warrior will fight to keep, and even increase, America's vast power. Why? Because T-Warriors understand that the

United States is a righteous country that has in our brief history freed billions of people from political enslavement. It was our might and money that brought down Tojo, Hitler, and the Soviet Union. As with all nations, America has obviously made mistakes, but we are at our core a noble country in a world full of hatred and violence. If we go into decline, the world will be a much more dangerous place. Can you picture Russia and communist China dominating the world? How about the combined Arab states?

But you'll **never** convince the committed secular-progressive warrior of America's nobility, and so the battle rages on. Traditionalists are fighting for their neighborhoods, their country, and their world. Since there's a huge amount at stake, the traditional cause must become a way of life. There are no "weekend warriors" in this culture war. We are in it to win it, which will require courage, commitment, and discipline.

It is now time to get back to basics; to develop a personal strategy designed to keep your family and country protected from those who would do us harm. And that strategy isn't all muscle and bluster. It requires incisive thought as well as action, two components key to the T-Warrior's ultimate victory.

Fifteen

The Code of the Traditional Warrior

> A Scholar Warrior is capable of perceiving right and wrong in an all too gray world and is just as capable of defending on the basis of that unstinting belief.
>
> —DENG MING-DAO

The Chinese philosophy of the Tao (pronounced "Dao" and meaning something like "the pathway") is a personal discipline that aspires to selfless, honorable living. The committed Taoist attains "Scholar-Warrior" status after much study and accomplishment in both the martial arts and "enlightened" thought. Because Taoists are definitely traditionalists, it may be useful to you to learn something of their culture. They believe in the dignity of humanity and adamantly oppose harming the innocent; thus terrorists need not apply. They also despise self-destruction, deceit, and the exploitation of others. Taoists form strong judgments about behavior and live by a strict code of right and wrong; thus moral relativists need not apply.

Although much different from the traditional warrior in his or her ultimate goals, the Scholar-Warrior has one thing all traditional warriors should have: a code to live by. This is extremely important, because if you can master a personal-life code of honor, you will not only develop the strength to influence others but also win many of the personal battles you will inevitably have to fight in this life.

For example, in my ten years of waging the culture war in the media, I have seen dishonest behavior from the S-P side almost every day of my life. Many of those people are rank liars and first-class manipulators. As I said in the beginning of this book, I truly despise the people who run the smear Web sites, or who use their positions in the media to injure rather than inform. I've described some of their behavior in this book, but believe me, I could write ten books about their disgraceful conduct.

Very important: Don't be like them. Some traditionalists (but more often fanatical conservatives) fall into the trap of using unethical tactics against the S-Ps. Don't you. The worse the S-P forces behave, the more noble you should strive to be. As I mentioned earlier, smear merchants play only to their choir. Fair-minded

Americans will not be persuaded either way by vicious personal attacks. Those are used by people who cannot win the debate intellectually.

So in this final chapter, let's discuss the righteous and somewhat rigorous code of the traditional warrior. I want to begin by pointing out that the code is the same for both women and men because women are some of the most effective T-Warriors. That might be because of child rearing; traditional women understand vividly how the S-P philosophy causes confusion and poor decision-making among kids. Of course, there are S-P moms out there like Susan Sarandon, but they are heavily outnumbered by traditional mothers. Thank God.

The cornerstone of the traditional warrior's code is to **do what you say you are going to do.** I've touched on that principle in my previous books, but it is vital for the traditionalist to understand that what you **do**, not what you **say**, defines you. Each day of your life should be devoted to fulfilling your responsibilities right down to the most insignificant. Even if it's a little thing like saying you'll call somebody, well, call them. Don't say stuff and then not do it. That's sloppiness of character, and it can become habit-forming. It is very important for the T-Warrior to be a person of honor, to be a "standup" guy or gal.

What does that mean? Well, by being "standup," you tell the truth and defend your principles in public—even if they are unpopular. Now, you don't have to become a Jehovah's Witness going door-to-door, but what you say should always mean something when you do decide to speak. Think about it. There is nothing worse than going to a place like Los Angeles and having people say "Let's do lunch, babe." Is there anything worse than that? I don't know of one T-Warrior who's ever said anything like that. But plenty of S-Ps have. It's the dead giveaway of a creep. Rejecting phony jargon is yet another reason to leap over to the traditional side.

But seriously, if you tell somebody you'll do something—do it. People who honor their commitments and reject B.S. are **impressive** people. They actually stand for something. They stand for their word. No matter what they do for a living, their lives have meaning.

So the traditional code starts with you, the T-Warrior, doing what you say you'll do. Simple, but powerful.

And then there's the daily fight against selfishness, an essential rule of the code. Unlike the S-P acolyte who worships at the altar of "self-fulfillment" and often looks to other people (the government) to make that happen, the traditionalist tries to help others before pursuing personal gratification. As the Tao philosophy teaches, selfishness destroys compassion for one's fellow human beings and leads to greed and mistrust. It is ironic that the S-P philosophy of "humanism" (a secular emphasis on the needs of human beings) leads them to embrace lenient criminal penalties for violent offenders, the destruction of fetuses/babies in the abortion process, and a permissive view of substance abuse that corrodes body and soul. The traditionalist understands that true feeling for others requires a helping hand that leads to problem solving—not the collapse of standards that would make it easier for people to destroy themselves and others.

T-Warrior alert: Withstanding selfish impulses is a large part of the traditional code.

Next, the effective T-Warrior has to see the world the way it **really** is. Yes, this can be downright painful. Every human being has a tendency to indulge the impulse of wish fulfillment. We want that attractive person to be good and decent even though he or she is not. We want that role model to be flawless even though, at times, everybody commits errors. Sometimes, our most fundamental preconceived notions turn out to be dead wrong. In those cases, we have to be disciplined and smart enough to admit it.

The stringently disciplined T-Warrior must be a persuader, not a "Kool-Aid drinker." If you watch or listen to my programs, you know I use that phrase a lot. It is inspired by a cult leader named Jim Jones, who in 1978 convinced almost 1,000 people to commit mass suicide by drinking a poisoned Kool-Aid-type drink in the country of Guyana. Those poor souls would do anything Jones told them to do. They had no minds of their own and, after drinking the cyanide and Valium-laced drink, no breathing bodies either. Thus, I use the term "Kool-Aid drinkers" to describe people who blindly follow any ideology or religion.

That's not the T-Warrior. In order to be effective, we must have our eyes wide open at all times. Things change quickly in America; for that reason, no one ideology or belief system can be correct in every matter. The clearheaded warrior who uses fact-based arguments rather than boring mantras (Bush lied) will win people over. As I've mentioned, the zombie-like, hateful warrior who spouts clichéd propaganda will drive reasonable folks away. All fanatics hurt whatever causes they are attached to. Don't be like Mike (Moore), looking to create or distort situations to fit your ideology. Don't be a Savage, selling hate as entertainment. No, see the world the way it is and try to apply traditional thinking to solve vexing problems. That is the road to victory.

The next aspect of the traditional code is vital: Stand up for your country! You can't be part of the traditional force unless you truly believe the United States is a noble nation. And, if you study history and look around you, that is not a difficult conclusion to reach. Why do millions of people from all over the world attempt to get into America any way they can? At least 12 million undocumented aliens live in the United States right now. Why do most American citizens have more opportunity than do our peers in the rest of the world? Why are you free to do pretty much whatever you want this evening?

The answer is freedom and a social structure that allows the intense pursuit of happiness for responsible, hardworking people. I am the poster boy for that truth about American life. As I was growing up, many in my Levittown neighborhood thought I'd eventually do time in Attica prison. Really. But I eventually wised up, worked hard, established a traditional belief system, and was able to reach my potential. If I can do it with my rather questionable personality, believe me, almost anyone can! I'm not a popinjay, but I can come darn close.

As a traditional warrior, therefore, I clearly understand from experience that my country has given me an opportunity to prosper. As much as I love Ireland, the land of my forebears, I don't believe I would have succeeded on a grand scale there. The opportunities in America are far more diversified than they are in Ireland or, for that matter, anywhere else on the planet. If you are tough and persistent, you will get a number of chances to succeed.

So I do truly respect my country and do not, like some of my S-P opponents you've met in this book, believe it is an evil, oppressive enterprise. I do understand that some corporations are brutal, but at the same time many American companies also provide life-sustaining benefits and opportunities for millions of people. True freedom means choosing between worthy enterprises and exploitative ones. There is definitely a dark side to the United States, but the T-Warrior learns how to put that truth in perspective. After all, there is definitely far more light than darkness in America, and you are free to walk away from most pernicious situations.

But excuses walk. To be effective in the art of persuasion, T-Warriors also must recognize that the United States has made mistakes in both domestic and foreign policy. Again, that's a small part of the overall picture, but it's there. T-Warriors are not an "America right or wrong" group. In my lifetime, the basic desire of the American government has been to provide people with freedom and the opportunity to better themselves. Even in Iraq and Vietnam, Americans fought on the side of freedom. So the downside of the United States is minuscule compared to what is noble about the country. That belief is a hallmark of the traditional warrior. We can certainly improve the United States, but if you want a completely different landscape, I am your ardent opponent.

For the next element of the code, I'm suggesting an unemotional examination of religion. This may come as a surprise to some, but you do not have to believe in God to be a traditional warrior, although the vast majority of us do acknowledge a higher power. But the code as far as religion is concerned is secular. Here's the twist: T-Warriors believe that the United States was founded on Judeo-Christian **principles** that have provided a foundation for freedom and justice.

The revisionist secular-progressive historians run around claiming the Founding Fathers were not at all influenced by Judeo-Christian philosophy, that their intent was to create a country where spirituality was a private matter. That is absolute nonsense, pure and simple. Just read the words of the Declaration of Independence and you'll see that the revisionists are lying.

The Founders wanted to construct a "God-fearing" country for very practical reasons. They knew the infant federal government couldn't control the growing population and, therefore, counted on the influence of Judeo-Christian tenets to keep the first Americans in line. Remember, in the initial days of the republic, folks largely policed themselves and established local order based upon widely accepted beliefs. There was no supposed "separation of church and state." That immense piece of false but effective propaganda was dumped on America in the late twentieth century by the ACLU. The only demand the Founders made in the religious arena was that no American legal apparatus could **force** a citizen to believe or worship in a certain way. Otherwise, the Founders encouraged public prayer, spiritual holidays, and a strong public belief in a benevolent Creator. That is the God's honest truth (sorry, S-P fanatics), and I can back it up all day long simply by pointing to public documents that are on display in the Smithsonian.

Now back to the code. . . . The traditional culture warrior understands that a clear definition of right and wrong is imperative for a disciplined society that protects its citizenry. One of the outrages of modern America is the S-P philosophy of confronting harmful behavior by providing a variety of excuses for it. For example, the "abuse excuse," whereby criminals become objects of sympathy because they, themselves, were abused, has taken deep root in the United States. As I explained earlier in these pages, we are now seeing the most repulsive acts, like the rape of children, being "understood." Instead of harsh punishment for child abusers, some judges are opting for lenient sentences and the option of "treatment" for felons who destroy kids. This is the most egregious example I can provide of secular-progressive "justice." Almost 100 percent of the time, the politicians, lawyers, and media who oppose strict mandatory sentences for child sexual predators are banner-waving soldiers in the S-P camp.

By contrast, the traditional culture warrior believes in the Judeo-Christian code of forgiveness—but with punishment and with penance. True justice demands that the punishment fit the crime. We in America must continue to uphold standards of behavior that protect people, especially children and the elderly, from harm. Civilized conduct is not "relative." In the American republic, the people decide what acts are wrong (illegal), and those acts must be punished accordingly. That code of justice, historically based upon Judeo-Christian principles, is one the S-Ps would tear down. Traditional warriors must prevent that from ever happening.

The traditional code goes on to include respect for private property. This is another core issue. I remember once asking the S-P actor Warren Beatty, a very smart guy, if he believed in "income redistribution." Beatty answered that he very much did. He favors allowing bureaucrats and politicians to remove money from the affluent (including himself) and then give it to others less well off.

As we've discussed, the secular-progressive belief that the government, not the American citizen, should hold ultimate power over private property is one of the most dangerous aspects of the secular-progressive agenda. This is what the slogan "tax cuts for the rich" is all about, a way of suggesting that reduced taxes for all Americans is somehow a kind of theft from low-wage earners. Similarly, the concept of "eminent domain"—the government's seizure of private property for the "greater public good"—is a stark indication of the S-P desire for centralized control of private property.

Simply put, traditional warriors will **defend**

private property. If you've paid taxes on your money, your land, your home, your stuff . . . then it should be yours forever. No pinhead public official should be able to take it away from you. That is why the so-called death tax is an abomination. After an American dies, Congress has deemed it can seize more than half of the deceased person's property if he or she is wealthy. I believe that is stunningly un-Constitutional, and it certainly is a very swift redistribution of wealth.

In defense of such actions, the S-Ps will point to the right of taxation written into the Constitution. And it is an easy play to convince most voters that the "rich" should pay the vast amount of taxes in America. After all, the "rich" have much more than most Americans will ever have. So who's going to feel sorry for them?

No one—and no one should. As a wealthy person, I believe I have a responsibility to pay more of my earnings in taxes than most other Americans pay, and also to give large amounts of money to charitable causes. I have no problem with that, unless the taxation becomes punitive or is repeated, as it is in the death-tax situation.

Let's be brutally honest here. T-Warriors simply do not believe in social engineering and income redistribution. I feel it is morally wrong for a distant government agency to take my hard-earned money and hand it over to someone else unless the person is simply not capable of caring for him- or herself. Once again, if we want to turn America into a socialistic republic, let's vote on it. But this "tax the rich" mantra is getting out of control. Socialism has never worked anywhere in the world, and traditionalists understand that.

But the secular-progressives don't care. They want "economic equality." It is amusing to watch mass demonstrations in France every time the hapless government there tries to institute new work rules. As stated earlier, the French government recently passed a new law that would allow companies to fire new employees under the age of twenty-six during the first two years of their employment. The authorities came up with that policy because the economy of France is moribund. No growth at all. That's because companies don't want to hire young workers knowing they can't fire them no matter how useless they turn out to be.

Naturally, the S-Ps in France took to the streets in protest because they love that kind of worker protection, even when it results in economic stagnation, which it inevitably does. And naturally French president Jacques Chirac, a champion of S-P thinking, backed down. France rescinded the new law.

In America, traditional warriors must fight against the government's running the economy and regulating what people earn. The United States has dominated the world economically because we the people are ambitious and are free to move up the economic ladder if we work hard and experience a bit of luck now and then. The S-P vision is that the nanny state will dictate what we have—and it will be based on "broad prosperity." That's S-P code for a guaranteed government-provided lifestyle—something the young French can't do without.

If you oppose that government guarantee, you will be branded "insensitive" and "hostile" to the workingman and to the poor. But the truth is that the code of the traditional warrior encourages generosity, philanthropy, compassion, and moderation in the pursuit of material things. However, it rejects the seizure of private property and the looting of the affluent. Class warfare is a strategy the S-P forces use very well. But that warfare goes against what America was founded on: the freedom to compete in the marketplace without governmental interference. Personal ambition has strengthened America and led to incredible opportunities for hundreds of millions of people. The traditional warrior understands that and rejects the voodoo economics of the income redistributors. It didn't work for Fidel or the Sandinistas, and it won't work for the S-Ps.

So, as you can see, the code of the culture warrior encompasses many things: ethical behavior, theory, spirituality, a realistic worldview, and a determination to fight for the soul of your country. Obviously, full engagement in the culture war demands energy and commitment, courage and persistence. You will be challenged; you may even be attacked and threatened. This culture war is not for the timid.

Traditional preparation for a shooting war requires a strict physical regimen to build up stamina and strength. If you've served in the military, you know how difficult basic training can be. You build up your body and mind to absorb whatever the enemy will throw at you.

Training to fight the culture war requires more mind than body work, and it's not just about absorbing knowledge, although that is very important. It's also about adopting an ethical life philosophy. As Deng Ming-Dao writes: "It takes a strong person to be ethical, for ethics are standards you may decide to follow even when others do not agree. Unless you are completely in control of your life and have a great deal of discipline, you cannot be ethical."

That's what separates the traditional warrior from his or her S-P counterpart—that strong emphasis on personal discipline and control of your actions. While the S-P corps practices "relativism" and theorizes about "nurturing" everyone (including the most horrendous among us), the T-Warrior chooses a belief system that realistically benefits society as a whole and tries to implement it with fairness and compassion. T-Warriors do make judgments, but based only upon strong evidence. T-Warriors believe society must protect the weak and look out for individual rights, but strictly within a framework of emphasizing personal responsibility and accountability.

While the S-P brigades clamor for legalized drugs, unfettered destruction of human fetuses, euthanasia, rehabilitation instead of criminal punishment, vastly more freedom for minors, parity for alternative lifestyles, forced sharing of personal assets, a "one world" consensus on foreign policy, banishment of spirituality from the marketplace, and other "enlightened" social policies, the T-Warrior understands the erosion of societal discipline that those policies would cause and, thus, rejects them.

But T-Warriors are not just naysayers. Like the Taoist "Scholar-Warrior," we are champions, defenders, and protectors of a noble country and of people worldwide who are decent, well-intentioned, and generous. T-Warriors adamantly support something that has succeeded for 230 years: the American Constitutional concept of freedom and justice that allows individuals to prosper and help others.

So there you have it—the code of the traditional warrior. To review, let's break it down into ten pithy segments:

- Keep your promises.
- Focus on other people, not yourself.
- See the world the way it is, not the way you want it to be.
- Understand and respect Judeo-Christian philosophy.
- Respect the nobility of America.
- Allow yourself to make fact-based judgments.
- Respect and defend private property.
- Develop mental toughness.
- Defend the weak and vulnerable.
- Engage the secular-progressive opposition in a straightforward and honest manner.

Words for all T-Warriors to live by.

Central Command (CENTCOM): Final Mission Statement

Life is tough. You know that. There are people you love and people you loathe. Every day of your life bad things happen, but the strong person soldiers on and consistently turns negatives into positives.

Sometimes—it's true—I wish I were not a traditional warrior. The fight is hard and exhausting. If you've followed my career at all, you know I have become a major target. Believe me, things were a lot easier when I was running around the globe reporting news stories. I'm not complaining, just bloviating (a little). As I've shown, I have taken on some very powerful interests in the United States and they are not at all pleased.

It's been ten years now since I began this fight. Mostly, I have won. My programs are hugely successful, my books are bestsellers. But I've paid the price, and so have those around me, because the amount of hatred directed my way is staggering.

Still, I have chosen my own path and do not regret it. A decade ago, the Fox Newschannel and **The Factor** did not exist. Think about what America would be like now if we had not arrived on the scene and provided Americans with an alternative to the strongly S-P established media. Over that same span of time, the secular-progressive movement has acquired a tremendous amount of money and power. They do not yet own the hearts and minds of most Americans, but they do have the resources, especially by controlling the media, to change that situation. So each American has to figure this out and understand that today's culture war, along with the war against terror, will define this country for decades—and maybe generations—to come.

Think about all the changes you've seen in your lifetime. My grandparents were born in a time when even cars did not exist! The amount of progress we've all seen is incredible. As with most things, some of that change has been terrific and some of it horrific. Therefore, it is our commitment as T-Warriors to hold on to the good and destroy the bad. Because we do make judgments, traditional people are in a good position for that task, but only so long as our judgments are sound and based upon the true philosophy of America.

So that is the mandate of the mighty T-Warrior. I hope, as more and more Americans begin to understand what's at stake, that the traditional forces will grow in power and influence and we will win the culture war and win it quickly. This may be wishful thinking, but hey, traditionalists can "nurture" that kind of optimism, right?

But even if I'm wrong and the unthinkable happens—that is, the United States "evolves" into a secular-progressive country—I'll know that I have fought on the side of the angels. I will have fought the good fight, and will have fought it honestly. Also, I will always have insights the S-P legions will never have: There is a right and a wrong in this world. There is justice and fairness. And, finally, there is a strong, binding tradition that has made America the most successful country the world has ever seen.

Let's keep it that way. Thanks for reading this book.

Bill O'Reilly
Fall 2006

THE WHITE HOUSE
WASHINGTON

Christmas, 1943.

TO OUR VETERANS:

Now that we know in our hearts that ultimate victory is certain, we can face the long hard struggle ahead with confidence and fortitude and let the spirit of Christmas pervade our thoughts and bring us comfort and a measure of happiness. I know that I speak for the Nation, as well as myself, when I assure you of our gratitude for the service you so bravely and honorably rendered and of our continued solicitude for your welfare and contentment.

A Merry Christmas to each of you -- may the New Year be for you and yours a happy one.

Franklin D Roosevelt

Another Christmas message from a President leading our nation in wartime.

ACKNOWLEDGMENTS

Unlike many high-profile people, I write my books myself. But no one can complete a manuscript alone. My editor for many years, Charles Flowers, continues his brilliance in this publication. Broadway Books's best editor, Gerry Howard, keeps an eye on me and Flowers with style and wit.

Since I am incapable of negotiating a computer, my wife, Maureen, routinely stops my bad language and presses the buttons that need to be pressed. Also, Makeda Wubneh continues to provide me with the best research on earth.

My literary agent, Eric Simonoff, is a great sounding board, as is the top guy at Broadway, Steve Rubin. Thankfully, the boss at Fox News, Roger Ailes, continues to lend me perspective. Every time I tell Ailes that I have another idea for a book, he rolls his eyes. But he's always been supportive, and, obviously, that's a huge help.

My broadcast agent, Carole Cooper, also continues to help me in ways far too numerous to mention. No way could I complete a project like this without her help and counsel.

So that's the C-W team. And believe me, it's a winner.

PHOTOGRAPHY CREDITS

p. 44	Associated Press/AP
p. 51	Associated Press/AP
p. 56	Associated Press/AP
p. 63	CBS/Landov
p. 66	Getty Images
p. 74	Reuters/Fred Prouser/Landov
p. 78 (left)	Getty Images
p. 78 (middle)	Photofest
p. 78 (right)	Getty Images
p. 146	Getty Images
p. 186	Associated Press/AP
p. 216 (left)	Flip Schulke/Corbis
p. 216 (right)	Associated Press/AP
p. 222	Photo by David Fisher/Rex Features, courtesy Everett Collection
p. 229	Nicolas Guerin/Azimuts/Corbis
p. 283	Associated Press/AP

INDEX

Page numbers in **bold** refer to illustrations.

ABOUT THE AUTHOR

BILL O'REILLY, a two-time Emmy Award winner for excellence in reporting, is a thirty-year veteran of the television industry. He served as national correspondent for ABC News and as anchor of the nationally syndicated newsmagazine program **Inside Edition** before joining Fox News, where he is currently executive editor and anchor of his own prime-time news program, **The O'Reilly Factor.** He is the author of the megabestsellers **The O'Reilly Factor, The No Spin Zone,** and **Who's Looking Out for You?,** as well as **The O'Reilly Factor for Kids** (with coauthor Charles Flowers) and the novel **Those Who Trespass.** He holds a master's degree in public administration from Harvard's Kennedy School of Government and a master's degree in broadcast journalism from Boston University.